OXFORDSHIRE GHOSTS

Oxfordshire Ghosts

by
Joe Robinson

Wharncliffe Books

DEDICATED TO

Luke and Daniel, Those Lovers of the Mysterious.

First Published in 2000 by
Wharncliffe Books
an imprint of
Pen and Sword Books Limited,
47 Church Street, Barnsley,
South Yorkshire. S70 2AS

Copyright © Joe Robinson 2000

For up-to-date information on other titles produced under the
Wharncliffe imprint, please telephone or write to:

> **Wharncliffe Books**
> **FREEPOST**
> **47 Church Street**
> **Barnsley**
> **South Yorkshire S70 2BR**
> **Telephone (24 hours): 01226 - 734555**

ISBN: 1-871647-76-2

A CIP catalogue record of this book is available from the
British Library

Cover design: Wharncliffe Books.

Printed in Great Britain by
Redwood Books, Trowbridge, Wiltshire

CONTENTS

Introduction

Don't we all just love a mystery? What happened to Shergar, is Lord Lucan still alive, are there aliens, I think I saw Elvis at McDonald's etc etc. The list is endless, perhaps the greatest mystery of all is,"Is there life after death?"

I have certainly had to change my ideas regarding the hereafter. Too many honest intelligent people have absolute belief that there is, "Something out there", following what can only be described as a 'spiritual' experience.

One or two mysteries close to home may help illustrate that, despite extreme cynicism from the scientific community, there is still a world of 'another kind' which we are unable to understand or . explain.

The Little People

Ancient implements and tools associated with leathercraft, carpentry and agriculture, have been unearthed in several parts of the United Kingdom and Ireland.

On their own these finds are not unusual, until the significance of the discoveries fully impacts upon that which we accept as normal, for these implements were so minute, that it was at first considered that they had to be children's playthings. .

It was several years after the first discovery in Cornwall, that a detailed examination of a number of the tiny implements was carried out and to the absolute amazement of researchers, it was discovered that in many cases they were inscribed with intricate patterns. It was further discovered that there were clear signs of wear and tear which could only have been caused through continuous and regular use.

It was only through the introduction of a new and very powerful microscope that a research programme to discover the origin of the tools revealed that they were not children's toys, but implements which carried all the signs of having been the everyday working tools of tiny artisans, resident in some numbers in various parts of Britain.

Giants

Jack the giant killer is a much loved fairy tale set in Cornwall, or is it a fairy tale? Whilst renovation work was being carried out at St Michael's Mount near Penzance, the skeletal remains of an extremely tall man were discovered, three metres in height the skeleton revealed a blow to the skull which most probably led to his death. The story in that part of Cornwall is that a local youth named Jack, rather than accede to the tyrannical demands of the giant, met and slew him on the causeway leading to St Michael's Mount.

The Kings Standing Giant

Nearer home, not far from Witney, at Kings Standing, opposite the Ascott under Wychwood turn, the skeleton of a man approaching three metres in height was found in a shallow grave. All indication were that this giant had been slain in a ritualistic manner and buried very close to a ley line.

Fairies

On two occasions elves, fairies or manikins, perfectly formed but no more than eight inches in height, have been discovered as far apart as the New Forest and close by Wychwood Forest. The New Forest 'fairy', was discovered in a large bin containing logs for the fire, the Wychwood 'elf' was found in a shed at Leafield, both it seems, had sought shelter during a particularly harsh winter. The foregoing are just a few of the many strange happenings on an earthly plane, if such things have happened and been recorded, then might there not be even more startling occurrences on an unearthly plane?

Read on and judge for yourself.

West Oxfordshire is a region rich in history and with more than its fair share of places both mystical and spiritual, landscapes of the past can be discovered in the ancient buildings and ruins located within Witney and the surrounding area.

'Wychwood the secret forest', protected for hundreds of years still retains its secrets Witney's link with the last Saxon king of England can be discovered in the story of Queen Emma and the 'fiery ordeal' which connects her to the Bishop of Winchester's Palace, now a haunted ruin. Akeman Street that great 'Roman motorway', runs through the region and the Roman legacy can be observed in the many encampments round and about Witney. Minster Lovell ruins housed one of the most influential families in England, a family brought to grief by Lord Francis Lovell, who's ghost now haunts the remains of that beautiful Baronial mansion.

Ley-lines

Ley-lines, those mysterious magnetic runs, flow through West Oxfordshire. Associated with the ancient mystics, the 'Old Straight Tracks' may well account for the many haunted places in the district.

Within a few miles of Witney are three further ancient sites, the place where St George killed the dragon, Rollright Stones and the Uffington White Horse, all places associated with the medieval belief in the devil and his ability to meddle and wreak havoc in human affairs.

With the exception of two obvious 'tongue in cheek' stories all tales related within the book are the genuine experiences of West Oxfordshire folk.

THE HAUNTED TRIANGLE

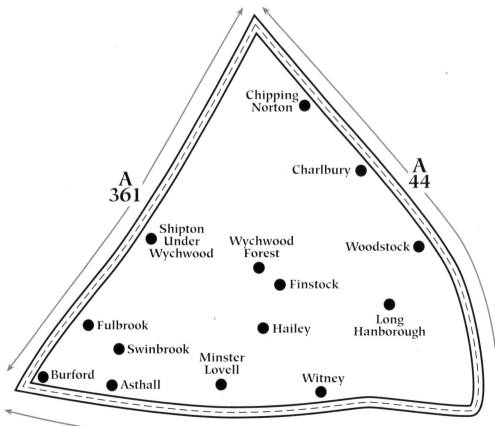

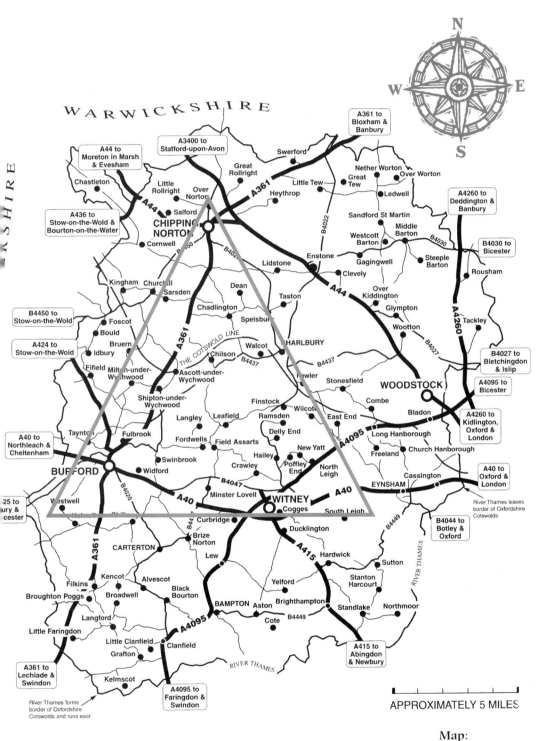

District map by kind permission of West
Oxfordshire Tourist Board.

Map:
Property of West
Oxfordshire Tourism.

CHAPTER ONE

SUPERNATURAL EVENTS IN:
MINSTER LOVELL AND WYCHWOOD

If it is to be judged on population alone, the village of Minster Lovell would be in the top ten of the most haunted places in England. Lying about two miles above Witney on the banks of the river Windrush, Minster houses a church and the ruins of an ancient baronial mansion, once home to the Lovells. Exquisite in its setting, the Hall has a mystical fairy-like quality, with Akeman Street, that old Roman Road, no more than a mile to the north; it is little wonder that this place, steeped in ancient history and legend, still plays host to knights and maidens, long since dead.

A lovely autumn day shot of St Kenelms Church, Minster Lovell.
Photograph of St. Kenelms Church by kind permission of FR. Adrian Gabb-Jones.

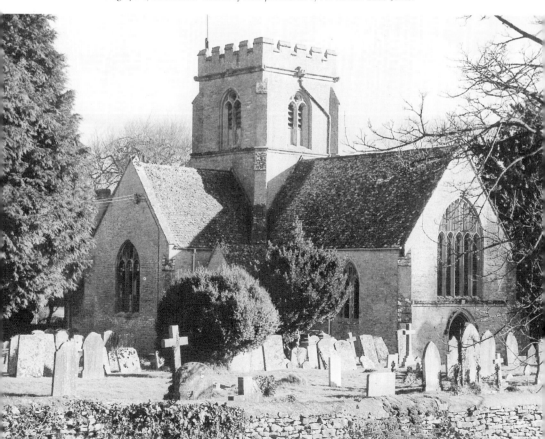

Minster Lovell map by kind permission of Barrie Rogers.

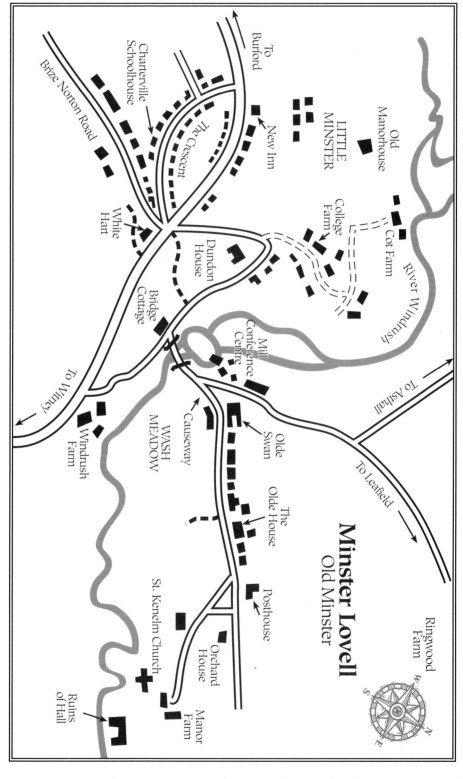

To Burford

Charterville Schoolhouse

The Crescent

Brize Norton Road

New Inn

LITTLE MINSTER

Old Manorhouse

River Windrush

To Asthall

College Farm

Cot Farm

White Hart

Dundon House

Bridge Cottage

Mill Conference Centre

To Leafield

To Witney

Windrush Farm

WASH MEADOW

Causeway

Olde Swan

The Olde House

Minster Lovell
Old Minster

Ringwood Farm

Posthouse

St. Kenelm Church

Orchard House

Manor Farm

Ruins of Hall

Minster Lovell village derives its name from two sources, Minster, a church served by secular priests and Lovell from the family who settled there in the late thirteenth century. The church was built and dedicated to prince Kenelm, a son of Kenwulf, King of Mercia. Prince Kenelm is widely believed to have been murdered in AD819 at Halesowen, in what is now the west Midlands, therefore the original church or Minster would have been built during the early part of the ninth century. The name Lovell became attached to the Minster in the thirteenth century, this was necessary to distinguish it from the nearby manor of Little Minster, part of the Earl of Pembroke's estates.

It is probable that William Lupellos, the first Lovell, received Minster from Henry I in or around 1125. William was the grandson of Robert, Lord de Brecherval, who arrived with William the Conqueror, the de Brechervals were originally from Ivry in Normandy.

The present ruins are all that remains of the manor house built between 1422 and 1437 by William, seventh Baron Lovell of Tichmarsh, descendant of John Lovell who married Maud, heiress of Robert, Lord Holand of Tichmarsh. John de Lovell was ennobled as the first Baron by Edward I and from then until the defeat of Richard III at Bosworth Field, when Francis, Viscount Lovell, fled to Flanders, the Lovells were one of the most influential families in the land. That is but the briefest of glimpses into a fascinating period in the history of what is now a ruin, but which at one time, was home to the mighty.

Our story concerns Francis, Lord Lovell who, after fleeing to Flanders following Richard's defeat at Bosworth, returned to England, joined Lambert Simnell's partisans at the Battle of Stoke and following their defeat, disappeared into thin air, or so it seemed, until 1708 when during renovation work at Minster Lovell Hall, a secret room was discovered.

Following the Battle of Stoke and the defeat of Simnell's force, several stories circulated regarding the nature of Francis' death. One report had him slain on the field of battle. He was also reportedly drowned whilst attempting to cross the river Trent on horseback. Living or dead, Francis, Lord Lovell, was never seen again.

Another story which has persisted down through the years, had the young Lord Francis concealing himself in a cave or underground chamber. Further credence was given to this tale with the circulation of a rumour amongst the locals, that Francis had

Two evocative shots of Minster Lovell ruins. By kind permission of English Heritage.

actually been hiding in a secret vault within Minster Lovell Hall, when the only access point was 'walled up'. The one person aware of the hiding place had died and thus consigned the noble Lord to a grisly end indeed. It is generally accepted that the strange sightings in and around Minster ruins are connected with Francis Lovell, who, seemingly did manage to cross the river Trent, following the Battle of Stoke, and eventually returned to his ancestral home. A party of American tourists from Ohio witnessed and described the following.

Time Slip?

Four of our party had arranged to stay in Witney overnight. We were part of a large group visiting the UK on a Beatrix Potter/ Literary Tour. The other members of the tour group had carried on to Stratford upon Avon, but we four had been invited to stay overnight at the house of a pen friend, intending to re-join our party the following day.

Our host arranged for us to visit the ruins at Minster Lovell and this was to be followed by a drink at the 'Old Swan'. We weren't sure what to expect but were amazed when we saw what good condition everything appeared to be in, we expected a ruin, but instead we got a grand old mansion. The following description of their experiences was given, and apart from one or two minor details, all four ladies in the group agreed that they had each witnessed the same thing. It was approximately seven in the evening, the month was April and the year 1983. We were, all four of us, standing on a cobbled square in a large courtyard. To the front of us was a building with an open door, there were three large leaded windows, to the left of the door, and two windows about half their size to the right of it. There was a passage to the left which went back about thirty yards with more buildings at the end of this passage. It was difficult for us to see these buildings clearly.

The building directly in front of us must have had an upper floor or floors, as there were four smallish windows high up in the wall, which were arch shaped in plain glass with narrow panes, above the six ground floor windows. We could see the roof of what must have been a further building, immediately behind the one in front of us, it may have all been joined as one building but we couldn't be sure. The roof was about fifteen to twenty feet higher than that of the first building. There was a prominent tower on the right hand end, seemingly put there as an afterthought, this appeared to be five sided and attached to the larger building.

To our right, when we were facing the buildings, was a stone wall with an arched gateway, the wall was about six to seven feet high. Behind and to the left of the wall was a hotchpotch of buildings, however, our attention was attracted by a large horse covered in mud and lather walking slowly across the courtyard. It had leather protection on its chest and above it's front legs and was being led by an elderly man dressed in a dark brown short smock and what looked like grey hopsack leggings. Mounted on the horse was a man carrying a visored helmet, but still wearing a breastplate and chain mail armour. His hair was very long and dark and the whole impression of horse and rider was of complete exhaustion. The trio crossed from left to right and simply disappeared through the wall.

How the description of the buildings, as seen by the four ladies from Ohio, compare with any of the original buildings, bearing in mind there were at least three great houses on this site, I do not know. What I do know, however, is that we have four intelligent, articulate people all seeing buildings and people long since gone. Call it a vision or a time slip, call it what you may, nothing can shake the ladies' belief in the reality of what they witnessed that April day.

The knight on horseback as described by the four American ladies is strangely at variance with other sightings at Minster Lovell. The horse and rider are usually seen as a knight in full shining armour and mounted on a huge white warhorse and there have been numerous sightings of this so called 'White Knight'. It is not clear from the many descriptions available, as to who he is or which period he is from, but it is generally accepted that, because of the circumstances surrounding the death of Francis, Lord Lovell, that it is probably poor Francis still chained to an earthly home, until his spirit is released.

The White Lady of Minster
The exact marriage and subsequent death dates of the 'White Lady' is not known, but the events described are believed to have occurred in the mid seventeen hundreds. This is an exceedingly sad tale, starting out as a doubly happy event combining the Christmas festival with a marriage between youthful William Lovell and his beautiful young bride. Neither guests nor family could have been remotely aware of the tragedy about to unfold upon that beautiful crisp, winter day.

Following the marriage ceremony, bride, groom and guests were participating in the simple pleasures of the times; the music, dancing, a sumptuous feast, many valuable wedding gifts and a truly happy and joyous atmosphere, all added to the poignancy of what was about to unfold upon that fateful day.

Following the Wedding feast a game of hide and seek was suggested. All readily agreed and the young bride was chosen as the hare, she raced up the stairs and entered the turret room, there in the corner was a large chest, which was occasionally used for linen storage, the young bride clapped her hands with pleasure thinking that she would never be found, how true that thought turned out to be, upon entering the chest and closing the lid behind her the clasp engaged, effectively turning the chest into her tomb. Despite desperately searching the house and grounds, Lovell's bride could not be found, it was as though the girl had vanished into thin air. Lovell was distraught and driven to the point of madness, he was often seen during the following days, weeks

Ancient archway at Minster Lovell Hall. By kind permission of English Heritage.

The ruins of the once magnificent Minster Lovell Hall.
Photographs by kind permission of English Heritage.

months and eventually years, searching ever searching for his lost bride, the memories and the pain associated with that fateful day turned Lovell into a lonely, melancholic recluse.

It was approximately two years following the fateful event that the chest was discovered, opened, and there entombed in that wooden coffin were the remains of Lovell's bride. This whole sad tale inspired the Victorian poet Thomas Haynes Bayley to write,

THE MISTLETOE BOUGH

The mistletoe hung in the castle hall,
The holly branch shone on the old oak wall,
And the Barons retainers were blithe and gay,
And keeping their Christmas holiday.
The Baron beheld with a father's pride,
His beautiful child, young Lovell's bride,
While she with her bright eyes seem'd to be
The Star of the goodly company.
Oh! The mistletoe bough, Oh! The mistletoe bough.
'I'm weary of dancing now,' she cried;
'Here tarry a moment, I'll hide
And Lovell be sure thou'rt first to trace
The clue to my secret hiding place.'
Away she ran, and her friends began
Each tower to search and each nook to scan,
And Young Lovell cried 'Oh where dost thou hide?
I'm lonesome without thee, my own dear bride.'
Oh! Mistletoe bough, Oh! Mistletoe bough.
They sought her that night and they sought her next day
And they sought her again when a week passed away;
In the highest, the lowest, the loneliest spot
Young Lovell sought wildly but found her not.
And years flew by, and their grief at last
Was told as a sorrowful tale long past;
And when young Lovell appeared, the children cried,
'See, the old man weeps for his fairy bride.'
Oh! The mistletoe bough, Oh! The mistletoe bough.
At length, an old chest that long had laid hid
Was found in the castle, they raised the lid,
And a skeleton form lay mouldering there
In the bridal wreath of the lady fair.
Oh sad was her fate! In sportive jest
She hid from her lover in the old oak chest;

It closed with a spring, and her bridal bloom
Lay withering there in a living tomb.
Oh! mistletoe bough, Oh! mistletoe bough.

There appears to be little doubt that the young bride of Lovell is the 'White Lady' often seen in and around the ruins, usually at Christmas time.

There follows an account of an appearance by the 'White Lady', in September 1993 at between eight and eight thirty in the evening. The apparition was seen by Mr Ferguson, a resident of Witney and his companion, a relative visiting from Tyneside.

What follows is Mr Ferguson's account.

'I was with a relative from up North, who was holidaying with me for a week. He suggested we have a drive out into the country and as I did not wish to go very far, I opted for a visit to the Minster Lovell ruins followed by a drink at the 'Old Swan.' Having parked the car near the church we set off to walk to the ruins. It was a very pleasant evening, warm and still and we walked to the banks of the River Windrush, picking our way through the ruins. We had just turned to make our way back when we saw the 'White Lady.'

"The figure was that of a very young girl, the impression we got was she must have been between fourteen to at the most, sixteen years old. Her hair was long and dark and her head was encircled by a small garland of flowers. The dress she wore resembled a long night gown with a golden cord encircling her waist. The cord was held by a silver brooch or buckle with two ends of the cord falling away almost to her feet, the dress was white.

'My companion and I were about twenty five to thirty yards from the figure which was moving gracefully to just left of centre of what would have been the main hall. The white lady stopped and then moved upwards, mounting stairs that simply were not there. At a height of about fifteen feet, the figure disappeared into thin air.'

Not losing a second, we hurried to the point where the figure had stopped prior to ascending the non existent stairway. Apart from a cold chill emanating from the spot where the 'White Lady', had started her ascent, there was nothing to indicate that anything *unusual had occurred. Nothing can undermine our belief in what we witnessed that September evening, something extraordinary occurred and both my companion and I felt privileged to have witnessed it'.*

The actual chest in which 'The White Lady' perished, is at Greys Court, Rotherfield Greys, Henley, Oxfordshire. Greys Court is a National Trust property and open to the public. Greys Court was once in the possession of William, Seventh Lord Lovell.

THE HAUNTINGS WYCHWOOD

The small bridge crossing the river Windrush at Swinbrook, is the setting for a most unusual manifestation. A young woman clad in the garb of a mid fifteenth century gentlewoman, carrying a small bundle in her arms, walks onto the bridge, stops in the centre and slowly melts into nothingness before any observer who happens to

The bridge at Swinbrook, where the ghost of young Martha can still be encountered searching for her long dead child.

be present at the time. Though elegant, the woman's clothing is somewhat dirty and dishevelled, while she appears to be in considerable distress as she clings tightly to the obviously precious bundle in her arms. Despite much careful research, there is no known local incident which could have triggered such an apparition in this particular spot. There is however a folk tale originating nearby, which may well give the clearest indication for the reason behind the appearance of this frail, dishevelled and clearly desperate young woman.

The Witches of Wychwood, A Folk Tale
The weather vane atop the cottage chimney stood out starkly against the clear blue sky in the shape of a crouched black cat,

almost imperceptibly a slight breeze moved the vane, giving the impression of a real cat waiting to pounce. This cottage had allegedly been home to witches during the sixteenth century, or so local folk lore has it. As it happens, the stories handed down from one generation to the next in this tiny Cotswold village not far from Witney, contain a lot more than just a grain of truth.During the sixteenth century, the three women living at the cottage, two sisters and their aunt, were highly regarded as 'wise women'. Dispensing herbs, treating the sick, tending animals, they were generally regarded as good honest folk and an acceptable alternative to the nearest doctor, more than eight miles away.

The women were not local, having moved into the village seven years previously, and it was on the anniversary of their seventh year that a change in attitude began to take place among the three. Formerly sympathetic to anyone unable to pay for their services, the three would often accept produce, or an offer of help on their plot of land, as payment for treatment.

It was Martha Hussingtree, a scullery maid at the nearby manor house, who became the first villager to suffer at the hands of the three, following their change of outlook.

Martha, who was not overly endowed with intelligence and completely lacking in any form of education, had fallen pregnant to a married man. She was not the first young girl to become pregnant out of wedlock within that small claustrophobic community, but she would be the first to have a baby fathered by a married man. Martha had witnessed the punishment suffered by a friend who had delivered a bastard into the village, ostracised, openly spat at and generally reviled, the girl had attempted suicide and had only been saved from further attempts upon her own life, when the father of the child finally agreed to marry her. This had proven a ruinous undertaking for the girl's parents, who were obliged to endow half their land to the father, as part of the marriage contract. Martha was therefore aware of the fate awaiting her should she give birth to a married man's bastard, both her and her widowed mother's lives would be ruined, as instant dismissal for them both would follow should ever her mistress at the manor discover her secret.

Unable to confide in anyone within the village, Martha sought help from the only alternative source available to her, the three wise women. Martha made her way from the manor, hurrying across the lawn and nimbly leaping over the stepping stones fording the stream which ran through the grounds, crossing the river Windrush by the bridge, then walking along the riverside path which led to Wychwood forest. Along the forest path she went, over another bridge, and there on the edge of the village, stood the cottage home of the three women.

She nervously tapped on the door which opened almost immediately, to reveal the youngest of the three women. Accompanied by much stuttering and stammering, Martha's predicament was unfolded before the three women, who duly promised to help the distraught young girl. But it was also made clear that this help would be at a price. Martha's relief was instant and she promised that she would repay them in any way she could, fetching, carrying, anything, if only they would help her. The three ushered Martha out of the cottage, telling her to return in three days by which time they would have the solution to all her problems. Those were an interminable three days for young Martha, but eventually the time came for her once more to seek out the three women. Upon her arrival she was shown into a small darkened room, in which she noticed a not unpleasant smell, both heady and hypnotic. A cup of what was described to her as herb tea, was given to Martha and she was assured by the three that there was a way out of her difficulties. Not only could her secret be kept, but there would be a change for the better in her fortunes, should she accept their help. The choice put before Martha was a simple one, she either accepted help from the three, or prepared for a life of total misery for herself, the child she carried and her mother. Martha accepted and in accepting, she was bound by the conditions of 'The Pact', as surely as if she had appended her signature to a legal contract.

This was the beginning of a series of events which brought blackmail, devil worship and death to this once sleepy Cotswold village and which, four hundred and fifty years later, sees a young girl wandering soulless and lost, ever searching for her abandoned child. The three women living at Cat Cottage, were witches. All three were fully participating members of Lucifer's church and as such, their unending task was the conversion of as many souls as possible to Satan's cause. You could almost look upon them as sixteenth century missionaries, out to convert the heathen to Christianity. Only they were following the path of darkness.

At the heart of witchcraft is 'The Pact', with the Devil, the 'Maleficia', being the complete heresy which defines the difference between magic and sorcery. You may if you wish, practise either art, but a contract has to be drawn up with Satan himself, should you truly wish to practise the genuine black arts. Once signed, there is no possible means of escape from the terms of 'The Pact'.

The Pact

This 'Pact', defines the difference between magic and sorcery, both of which may be practised by men or women and independently of each other. However, for those who wish to fully participate in the black arts, it is necessary for the pact, or the 'Maleficia', to be drawn up between the individual neophyte practitioner and Satan.

The primary elements of the pact are that, upon the signature of the neophyte practitioner, an aspiring witch or warlock, Satan undertakes to satisfy all the earthly wishes and desires of the person concerned, in exchange for possession of their soul for eternity upon their death.

This contract is then attested in blood, by an already practising witch or warlock, following the signature of the neophyte. The circumstances surrounding this ceremony and the signing, leaves all parties in no possible doubt that, on completion of the signing the signatory is forever after, a creature of Satan.

Martha willingly entred into 'The Pact', initially out of terror, but she soon found herself gaining many material advantages which she could not have hoped to achieve by any other means. The man responsible for her pregnancy was also swiftly drawn into the growing coven, following threats to reveal all to his wife and family. His willing participation was soon secured when the possibility of sexual encounters with other coven members, allied to greater wealth and power was revealed to him.

By the time Martha was twenty four weeks pregnant, she cared little if the villagers knew or not. Her fortunes had changed beyond all recognition during the six months since she had entered into 'The Pact'. She had quit her job at the manor house and was now mistress of a flourishing business in the horse and carriage trade, with regular routes to Oxford and many other surrounding towns. Despite her pregnancy, she was also pursued by several young bachelors of the town who doubtless thought she would offer them a safe and very comfortable life, but Martha would have none of their advances and kept them all at more than arms length.

The membership of the coven had now grown to include twelve members, four being recruited personally by Martha, from among the young girls of the village. She was also instrumental in securing the membership of two further males, doubtless from among the many suitors who had been pursuing her.

The three witches of Cat Cottage had in fact been despatched from their founding coven in the Midlands to 'spread the gospel', and just as importantly, locate a suitable site for annual Sabbats. The Midland coven was one of the largest in the country, with over a hundred members, so the chosen site had to cater for a great many people of both sexes. Wychwood forest proved to be an ideal location and over the five years following the arrival of the witches in the village, an annual Sabbat had taken place there.

The Sabbat

It is assumed that Sabbats are held on specific dates, however this is not correct. A Sabbat may be held on any day and at any time, provided it is performed in a place properly prepared for the purpose. Clearly there will be certain times of the year or dates when the effectiveness of the ceremony is enhanced and these include, Candlemass, Spring Eve, The Winter Festivals and Lamas Day. On any of these festivals, the likelihood of the appearance of demonic entities or even Satan himself, are greatly enhanced.

Remote and with only a sparse population within its boundaries, Wychwood forest at the time we are discussing covered most of West Oxfordshire, giving limitless opportunity for discreet gatherings and secret ceremonies to be performed.

The forthcoming Sabbat was promised to be a particularly important one, as it was rumoured that it would include the sacrifice of a virgin. The key date of the twenty third of June was chosen as the most auspicious for this important ceremony, far more important than the more usual where a lamb, kid, or goat would fall victim to the sacrificial knife.

Martha was eight months pregnant on the day she was summoned to Cat Cottage and it was five days prior to the celebration of the Sabbat in the depths of Wychwood, planned for the twenty third of June. She was again introduced to the darkened room with its pleasant fragrances and sweet 'herbal tea', which the three women pressed upon her. As she relaxed upon the soft eiderdown laid upon the bed, Martha could hear the women talking softly among themselves, a sound which combined with the effects of the tea and perfumes was quite agreeable and relaxing. Later, the three witches assembled around the now drowsy Martha and the elder one whispered to her that, "Now my dear, 'tis time to repay thy master for the treasures he has given thee. You shall have thy child and bide here until the day of the Sabbat, when you shall see and hear such things as will lift your heart".

That night, Martha gave birth with such ease that she hardly knew she had delivered until she caught the soft sound of the cry of a new born infant, which was quickly hushed. The baby was immediately removed from her presence, her only indication even of its sex, was when one of the witches whispered to her that 'You'll only become attached to her and we don't want that now do we!'.

Genuine witches readily appreciate that all things have power, be they objects, trees, plants and most specifically, human beings. It is the harnessing of these powers which is essential for them to achieve the object of their spells. Therefore, access to and harnessing of the various sources of power with which our world abounds is essential for the success of any spell.

In Wychwood, on the twenty third of June, the place chosen for the performance of the Sabbat was being prepared.

The necessary symbols had been laid out. A huge pentagram, one of witchcraft's most significant and arguably most potent symbols, had been etched into the rich loam of the forest floor at the centre of the clearing, while black candles burned at the points and angles of the pentagram. Satanic law dictates that this symbol must be drawn with the left hand, indicating the left hand path of Satan's followers; it must also be started at the bottom and the top point left open while the whole lies within a broken circle drawn anti clockwise. It is believed that this extremely potent symbol which portrays the five prime elements, will attract all the powers of the dark forces to it.

The altar, comprising a heavy black stone slab standing upon two stone uprights, stood at the edge of the clearing in line with the open point of the pentagram. Upon the altar were two wooden bowls, one filled with water, the other empty and between them lay a silver knife.It was in this place and with this knife that the new born daughter of Martha Hussingtree was sacrified to the Lord of Darkness and during this ghastly ceremony, many claimed later that 'The Master', Satan himself made an appearance.

Two of the young girls whom Martha had lured into the coven and who were due to be initiated during the Sabbat, later gave chilling accounts of the sacrifice of the infant and their desperate escape from the awful scene. They claimed to have witnessed sights so horrifying, that they fled in terror and sought sanctuary in the local Church. Their confessions and a listing by them of all those they knew to be present at the Sabbat in Wychwood, bought their freedom for the price of the lives of five of their neighbours.

The three witches of Cat Cottage were also dragged from their home and summarily hanged, while Martha and the father of her child fled into the depths of Wychwood, but were later caught and also consigned to a scaffold built from Wychwood oak. Their corpses were then hung in a gibbett placed at the crossroads on the Asthalls to Leafield road.

It is said that Martha repented of her sins at the eleventh hour, thus saving her soul if not her earthly life. In truth it seems her punishment lingers on as she continues to search for her lost child, sacrificed to the Devil in the depths of Wychwood.

THE RETURN OF BLACKSTOCKINGS

On Moonlight nights, between Minster Lovell and Burford along what is now the old A40, near the turning to Asthall Leigh, just before the Windmill Restaurant, a notorious robber and highwayman known as 'Blackstockings', can be seen, sometimes on foot sometimes on horseback but always dressed in black. 'Blackstockings' adventures date from the 18th century.

There is no record of Blackstockings ever being arrested although several traps were laid for him and a large reward for his capture had been posted. It is now virtually certain that Blackstockings was a local man living around Worsham, he must have lived in that vicinity most of his life, for he appeared well acquainted with the area and utilised his local knowledge to plan his forays and evade capture. He appears to have been very meticulous in his planning.

In recent years, a young woman, whose father was the landlord of a local pub gave a dramatic account of a meeting with Blackstockings, following her return from a night out in Witney.

'It was two in the morning and I was on my way home from Witney to Fulbrook. I was in my car with a companion and had just passed Worsham Bottom, turned the bend and was half way up the hill on the A40 (now the B4047) when I received the fright of my life. There in the middle of the road was this figure all in black and mounted on a black horse, my lights were at full beam and there was no mistaking the fact that I was gazing at a highwayman. The figure on the horse appeared to be squat, he wore a tricorn hat and was brandishing a flintlock pistol, a cloak billowed around him and his horse kept rearing up on its hind legs. Fortunately for me my companion witnessed exactly the same things that I had; he later described in detail everything,

almost word for word, which I had described to my disbelieving parents.

As I approached this figure on horseback I started to brake, coming to a stop on the hill about ten to fifteen yards from the horse and rider, the figures were so real that I knew if I approached any closer the horse would either kick the car or I would be in danger of running into them. By now I was more angry and interested than frightened. I could clearly see the mask covering the rider's eyes and nose, the bottom half of his face was concealed by his cloak and he was holding an old

This illustration shows the point where the modern B4047 follows the same route as the 18th century road upon which 'Blackstockings' appears.

flintlock pistol in his left hand and the reins with his right. He wore shoes not riding boots, but black shoes; he had on black stockings into which black breeches disappeared, he was not wearing gloves nor could I see a ring on any of his fingers. The horse was jet black, almost as though it had been sprayed in glossy black paint; there was no gleam on any of the harness almost as though horse rider and harness had been sprayed in the same glossy black paint.

The car halted and apart from the sound of the engine and some very heavy breathing from my companion and I, there was not another sound. We both wound our windows down and leaned out, as we did this the rider spurred the horse, shoved the pistol into a holster or leather bag on the left side of the animal, wheeled to the right of the car and sped off without a sound, in the direction of Worsham Bottom.

I had never heard of any ghostly figures or phantoms appearing on that stretch of road before, but following this incident, the first I have ever experienced, my father mentioned it to the pub regulars who didn't think it strange at all, because Blackstockings has been a regular visitor to the area for many years.'

THE HITCH HIKER

There are areas on either side of Asthall Manor which are haunted, the apparition of a gypsy girl aged about twenty has been seen by several people, even more remarkable this phantom has also been picked up by two unsuspecting motorists. The carriageway which takes the traveller past the Manor, approximately two miles either way, is where the olive skinned gypsy-like figure is seen; she wears a peasant blouse and a loose fitting coat or cloak which billows around her. The following are the experiences of two people who have actually stopped, spoken to and given a lift to this strange phantom, a hitch hiker who when picked up is soaking wet and who subsequently disappears just as suddenly as she appeard.

Terry's Tale
October the seventh, nineteen ninety four, is a date that is etched in Terry's mind. On the night of the seventh he came into contact with a spectral figure and experienced what turned out to be the

most chilling event of his life. Terry is a senior sales executive working for a Japanese company based in the UK, so his work entails a lot of travel and he is an excellent driver and well used to all driving conditions. Those on the night of October 7 were normal for that time of year, rain had fallen but had now stopped and visibility was as good as could be expected. The journey home from his final visit of the day had brought him from Cheltenham and he was now no more that a few miles from home, five and a half miles to be exact, for as Terry puts it, 'every detail of that strange encounter is stamped and dated upon my mind'.

I was doing about fifty miles an hour when this green blob of light which was hovering left of centre of the road, suddenly took on the shape of a female, it was quite difficult to make out size and age because I was still about three hundred yards away from the figure, however, I knew without doubt that it was a woman. As I approached closer, braking and slowing down to ten miles an hour, I was able to make out her features. She was a young woman probably about twenty to twenty five years of age, she had dark shoulder length hair, her complexion was of a Mediterranean type, olive skinned, with deep brown eyes and she was carrying something.

The woman was waving frantically in the middle of the road and I had no alternative but to come to a complete halt or run her down; I lowered my window and asked, 'What's the trouble?' There was no reply and she walked round to the front passenger door, which I opened, she heaved a great sigh as she got into the car. The engine was still running and the interior of the car was warm, so I asked the woman again what the problem was and as she turned full face to me I could see she was dripping water all over the place, her dark hair was hanging in wet ringlets over her forehead and her clothing was soaked. It was as though this woman had just been dragged from the river. I said that we had better get her home sharpish otherwise she would die of pneumonia, but she pointed ahead, still without uttering a word, and I drove off. As I was driving I became aware of a terrible feeling of anxiety, it was awful, overpowering, as if I must get home at once or else something dreadful might happen; it was a physical thing there with me in the car. I had by now travelled half a mile, my speed was increasing in line with my overwhelming feeling of anxiety which was now mixed with a sense of despair, suddenly the woman uttered just five words to me, 'Its too late, he's gone', and with that she just simply disappeared, leaving no more than a slight misty haze within the car. I arrived home and it was obvious to my wife that something was wrong but

I couldn't bring myself to tell her what had happened. I simply told her that I had swerved to avoid an animal on the road and I was still a bit shaken.

Liz's Tale

I was on my way to Burford at three o'clock in the afternoon, intending to arrive in Burford by about three thirty to pick my son up from the church, where he was involved in an archaeological project organised by his school. It was raining, not heavily but sufficient to warrant an umbrella which I had in the back of the car, the date was March eighteenth, nineteen ninety five. Everything about that day seemed strange, it had an unreal, surreal quality. Although it is only a ten minute drive to Burford, from where I live, I decided to make an early start as I had suffered a couple of minor disasters in the house. The first arose from a leaking pipe in the cavity wall, this only became noticeable as a dark stain developed on the kitchen wall, then my washing machine managed to swamp the utility room floor. I thought it best not to take any further risks with picking my son up so I started out really early, when having travelled about two to three miles I came to the spot, where one of the most extraordinary things ever to happen to me occurred. A girl, well a young woman really, she looked like a gypsy, was standing in the middle of the road, just past Asthall Manor, waving frantically at me; she was soaked to the skin and as she was blocking the narrow stretch I had no option but to stop.

I wound down my window and before I could say anything she said, 'You got my message then', and she walked round to the passenger side of the car; I opened the car door and she got in. I was pretty dumbfounded by what was going on, but she was so obviously in a distressed state I felt I had to offer her help. I asked, 'What message? Where do you want to go? But she just sat there and gazed at me with such a tortured expression that I felt she must have experienced something really dreadful. I thought I must be dreaming this until the young woman simply said, 'The water, the river, he's gone', then she disappeared. All that remained to assure me that I wasn't dreaming and that someone had actually been in the car with me, was a pool of water, where her feet had been, and a soaking seat. I carried on to Burford, picked my son up and returned home via a different route. I have not until this disclosure, spoken of this incident to anyone.

I wonder how many unsuspecting travellers on that lonely stretch of road have seen or even perhaps given a lift to this phantom. What is she doing there and what awful experience keeps her spirit chained to that lonely carriageway?

CHAPTER TWO

SUPERNATURAL EVENTS IN:

WITNEY

I solated to the North by the great dark forest of Wychwood, and to the South by treacherous marshlands, it is not surprising that ancient beliefs and superstitions remained with the peoples of Witney long after Christianity had been introduced.

This very isolation helped create and form the character of these fiercely independent people, pitching them closer to nature. Educating them in the ways of the natural world and significantly, influencing them in their choice and form of whom and what they recognised as the great governing forces of their world. There is little doubt that Christianity was not as readily accepted by those secretive communities dwelling within the dark shadow of Wychwood forest, as it was by the townsfolk of England.

Accounts of ceremonies and rituals associated with the old lore have been passed down through the generations, it is therefore little wonder that this small area should have such a long standing and significant association with the supernatural.

Villages off the old A40 prior to the introduction of the Witney By-Pass. Old A40 is now B4047.

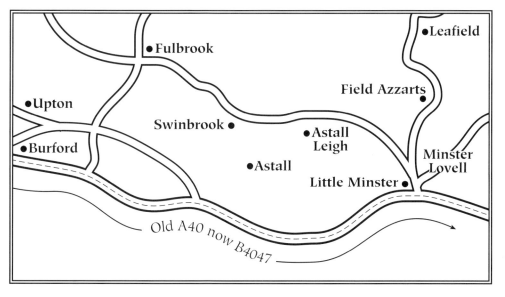

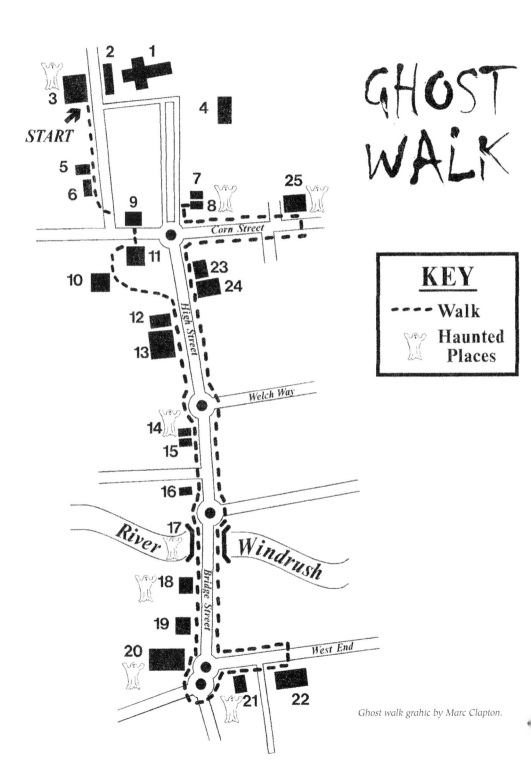

Ghost walk grahic by Marc Clapton.

GHOST WALK GUIDE

1. St Mary's Church
2. Holloways Almshouses
3. Bishop of Winchesters Palace
4. Henry Box School
5. St Mary's C of E Primary School
6. The Hermitage
7. Saltmarsh & Druce
8. 'The Angel'
9. The Buttercross
10. Corn Exchange
11. Town Hall
12. Cross Keys
13. Boots
14. Unwins
15. Weslyan Church
16. Blanket Makers Hall
17. The Bridge
18. 'Old White Hart'
19. Old County Court
20. Staple Hall
21. Jolly Tucker
22. 48 West End
23. Old Post Office
24. The Marlborough
25. Parliament House
    The Angel & Journeys End

Ghost Walk route by Marc Clapton.

THE WITNEY GHOST WALK

There is ample evidence of Witney's historic past, which a slow and pleasant stroll around this beautiful old Cotswold town will reveal. You will doubtless enjoy the delightful church of St. Mary, the ancient Buttercross, once a shrine to the Virgin Mary and the Bishop of Winchester's Palace where a host of kings, queens and minor royals once lodged. You may, if you are lucky and keep an open mind, also spot a ghost or two. Reminders of Witney's past are everywhere, both in our archaeological and spiritual heritage. Numerous ley lines run through the district and ghosts abound, for West Oxfordshire is probably the most haunted area in England. Here are just a few locations wherein you have the best chance of encountering ghosts both ancient and modern.

THE WITNEY GHOST WALK ROUTE

The walk starts at Church Green and the Bishop of Winchester's Palace, (Map ref: 3).

On Church Green you have an excellent view of St. Mary's church, (Map ref: 1), externally it is a beautiful building, while inside are many reminders of the ancient families of West Oxfordshire. The Wenman Chapel, built on the north west corner

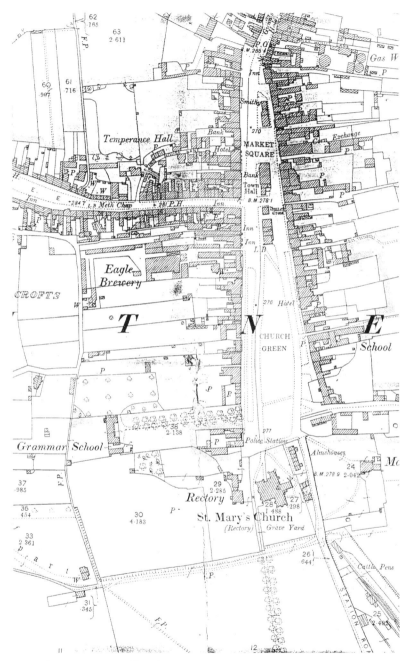

Map showing Witney Church Green in 1899.
By kind permission of Royal Ordnance Survey.

Church Green. *A splendid summer day view of Church Witney.*

of the church, commemorates the Wenman family, once one of the most notable families associated with Witney and the once flourishing wool trade.

Standing alongside St. Mary's are the Holloway's Almshouses, (Map ref 2), this row of cottages was gifted to the town by John Holloway in seventeen twenty four for the housing of six poor widows of the parish.

Leaving the Eleventh Century Bishop of Winchester's Palace, number three on the Ghost Walk map, we follow the route along

The Butter Cross and Town Hall. *Witney.*
Photographs by kind permission of Witney and District Historical Society.

A pre war view of High Street, Witney.

An early engraving of the Wesley Chapel, Witney.
Photographs and engraving by kind permission of Witney and District Historical Society.

Church Green, towards the town centre and the Butttercross. The Henry Box School, (Map ref: 4), is on your left as you walk toward the Buttercross. (Map ref: 9)

Henry Box, a local man, generously funded the building of this school in sixteen sixty three with profits made from his grocery business. Still on Church Green and on your right, is St Mary's Church of England primary school built in eighteen sixty, a fine Victorian building. (Map ref: 5) Again on your right is 'The Hermitage'. (Map ref:6) A Tudor building used by the Fellows of Merton College, Oxford as a place of refuge from the Great Plague of Sixteen Sixty Five. On the left hand side of Church Green, as you walk toward the Buttercross, can be seen the Angel Inn, (Map ref: 8) and your finishing point on the Ghost Walk, the Angel with its beautiful Georgian windows stands adjacent to Saltmarsh and Druce, (Map ref: 7), Witney's oldest and most respected grocers.

The walk has now taken us from Church Green and into Market Square where stands the Buttercross, (Map ref: 9), an ancient

Witney Grammar School soon after its completion.
Photographs by kind permission of Witney and District Historical Society.

columned monument around which controversy has raged for centuries. The exact history of this one time shrine to the Virgin Mary, is unknown. The Reformation witnessed the destruction of the shrine and the Buttercross site became a market-place for the sale of butter.

Also in Market Square is the Corn Exchange, (Map ref:10), built in eighteen sixty three, it is a fitting monument to the entrepreneurs who established Witney as a prosperous centre of the blanket industry. The seventeenth century Town Hall (Map ref: 11), occupies a prominent position in Market Square; it is an arched structure under which factors conducted their business buying and selling grain.

Moving northward into High Street you will pass the Cross Keys Inn, (Map ref:12), once a minor coaching inn.

Boots the Chemist (Map ref: 13), now occupies what was once the Old Temperance Hotel. Further down High Street and still on your right is Unwin's Wine Store, (Map ref: 14), which is number two on the Ghost Walk. Jack Kempster once ran a thriving music shop on these premises from 1930 to 1983, and prior to Jack Kempster the building was occupied by the Gas Coal and Coke Co.

The Weslyan Church, (Map ref: 15), in High Street, was opened for worship in eighteen fifty; there was, and still is a very strong Methodist community in Witney, quite probably as a result of many of the old mill owners insistence on their workers embracing Methodism!

Just beyond the Weslyan Church, and still in High Street, is the Blanket Makers' Hall, (Map ref: 16) built in seventeen hundred and twenty one, there is a most unusual one handed clock on the front of this building.

Dividing High Street from Bridge Street is the River Windrush, the waters of the Windrush flow beneath the bridge, (Map ref: 17), from which the street draws its name. This is Number Three in the Ghost Walk. This part of Witney was once a Saxon crossing place.

The current span replaced a hump backed bridge over the River Windrush, evidence of which can be seen by observing, at near pavement level, what was once a window on the first house immediately over the bridge.

Just beyond the bridge, and still on your right, is Number Four in the Ghost Walk the site of the Old White Hart, (Map ref: 18). The original buildings which housed this inn were incorporated into a blanket mill and they currently form part of a small business development. Number five in the Ghost Walk was formerly known as Staple Hall, (Map ref: 20), which is now a nursing home. To reach Staple Hall you must pass the old County Court, (Map ref: 19), finished and opened for business in eighteen fifty eight.

Staple Hall was one of the most important and largest staging posts and inns, on the London to Wales route. The Hall is understood to have originally been built during the fourteenth century. This ancient building was, to all intents and purposes, totally re-built in the sixteen fifties. Crossing Bridge Street into West End we now view where once the 'Jolly Tucker', (Map ref: 21), ale house stood in the somewhat unromantically entitled 'Pigs Head Square'.

For many years, a rich annual event was held in the ale house, it was known as the 'Tuckers' Feast', at which ''Tis Wonderfully Curious', would be sung by a chosen Tucker. The Post Office (Map ref: 21), now occupies the spot where the 'Jolly Tucker' once stood.

Not part of the Ghost Walk, but well worth recording, is number forty eight West End, the inspiration for the First World War smash hit 'The Old fashioned Town' this song was as popular in its day as any of today's 'top ten', hits.

Back into Bridge street, once again over the bridge and on into High Street, walking up Hill Rise you can see the Old Post Office (Map ref: 23), built circa seventeen fifty, and Witney's premier hotel 'The Marlborough' (Map ref: 24). This hotel has been re-developed and is a remarkable example of how a building can be modernised without destroying its ancient character. In this case a hostelry which is approaching its three hundredth birthday.

Turning right into Corn street we find ourselves in a stately and pleasant avenue. During the nineteen fifties, Corn street had the reputation of having more public houses within its length than any other street in Great Britain. In those days, Witney was famous for its 'Three Bs', Beer, Beauty and Blankets. On the corner of the Crofts and Corn street stands the mysterious building once known as the Parliament House, (Map ref: 25), which is number seven on The Ghost Walk. The building is now in the possession of the Abbeyfield Society, and it has a very strange history. Known to contain at least one secret staircase which led to a room which had been deliberately boarded up, the building is also believed to have been a temporary home for Parliament under James 1.

Walk back along Corn Street and once again into Market Square, we have now reached our final destination 'Ghost Walk Eight', The Angel Inn, (Map ref: 8), a delightful place to stop, perhaps rest those weary limbs and indulge in a well earned drink.

Do however be very careful on which stool you choose to sit. Now read on for full accounts of the haunted places.

GHOST EVENT 1

THE BISHOP OF WINCHESTER'S PALACE AND THE PHANTOM QUEEN

Queen Emma, originally married to King Ethelred the Unready, gave birth to the last Saxon King of England, Edward the Confessor, at Islip in 1003.

This outstanding Queen deserves a far more prominent place in English history than she currently occupies. Daughter of Richard, Duke of Normandy. Emma, following the death of her first husband King Ethelred, married King Canute. Emma became mother to Hardicanute, who reigned as King of England for only a short period. Following his death, Edward 'The Confessor', became king, as a result of which, this strong willed and ambitious woman, became mother to two kings and wife to a further two.

Queen Emma's Dyke and Queen Emma's, the local primary school, are reminders of Emma's place in the history of Witney. A

The magnificent Queen Emm's Willow at Witney, in full summer foliage.

further reminder is the Bishop of Winchester's Palace,or what remains of it, situated in the grounds of The Mount House, (Map ref: 3). A huge amount of work has been carried out by Witney's Historical Society in establishing and revealing just what a tremendous building once stood in this place. Many visitors from far afield and indeed local people, often enquire as to why the Bishop of Winchester should have a palace built at Witney. There is no doubt that the church played a major part in the establishment of Witney as a township, and as prolific 'land grabbers', in that period, the property was most likely just another profitable church acquisition. We shall let the historians deal in the facts of the matter, what I intend here is to give the delightfully romanticised version of how the Bishop of Winchester's Palace came to be built in Witney, and why the ghost of Queen Emma haunts the grounds.

Robert, Bishop to King Edward the Confessor, was held in high esteem by the king, being both confidant, advisor and friend. Robert, who later became Archbishop of Canterbury, jealously guarded his position as 'king's favourite'. The one person who threatened Robert's place within Edward's circle was Queen Emma, the king's mother. Emma, an extremely strong character, did in fact wield enormous influence over the court. In order to remove a perceived threat, Robert accused Queen Emma of two horrific crimes; he not only falsely accused Emma of murdering Alfred, the King's brother, but also of attempting to impede the King's succession to the throne. As a result of these accusations, King Edward ordered the convening of a synod, before which Queen Emma stood trial, the findings of the synod were that Emma should undergo 'Trial by Fiery Ordeal'. Following the decision of the synod, the Queen was taken to Winchester, and there in the nave of Winchester Cathedral, faced her ordeal.

Nine red hot plough-shares were placed within the nave, Emma's trial was to walk barefoot upon these implements. Her trial only ended when she had walked over the blistering plough-shares. The Queen survived the terrifying ordeal totally unscathed and thus was her innocence proved. In thanksgiving for her deliverance, the King, awarded the Bishop of Winchester twenty one manors, of which Witney was one and it was here that the Bishop built his Palace.

The Palace was sometimes utilised as a place of lodging for visiting royalty during their hunts in nearby Wychwood forest. Its construction was not completed until after the death of Queen

Emma, but tales have been carried down through the centuries, telling of Emma's haunting presence within the Mount House grounds. We cannot be certain that the Queenly figure seen floating by the beautiful willow tree, through what was once the moat, round the Palace ruins and finally disappearing through a fence is definitely the shade of Queen Emma, however her association with the romantic tale of the 'Fiery Ordeal', leads one to believe that it is indeed the shade of that formidable Queen, keeping an eye on her gift.

Several sightings have occurred of the ghost which haunts the grounds surrounding Mount House and the Palace. One of the strongest concerns a visitor to what used to be the offices of the tourist board, once situated at the Mount House. It was ten thirty on a grey October morning in nineteen ninety three when Peter Griffiths, representative of a Swedish paper group, was keeping an appointment to introduce his company's products to the tourist board staff. Peter had parked his car outside St Mary's church and was taking advantage of a twenty minute wait prior to his

The ruins of the once magnificent Bishop of Winchester's Palace, Witney.

appointment, he strolled around Church Green then slowly made his way along the gravel drive leading to the Mount House. He was half way along the drive, almost opposite the beautiful willow tree, when he was amazed to see, the upper part of what was unmistakably a lady, making its way from the willow tree, to what he later discovered was the ruin of the Bishop of Winchester's Palace. Whatever it was that Peter witnessed, swept past the tree, through a lawn and disappeared into the ruins; the whole sighting, according to Peter, lasting for no more than five seconds.

This intriguing sighting of what appears to be half a ghost, may not be so unusual, when one considers the circumstances. The Palace and the Mount House were built at widely different periods of history and the Palace was already a ruin and the moat had been filled in with the construction of the raised surround of the semi fortified House. Therefore, Peter would have seen a ghost which would have been following a route at the level formerly occupied by the Palace. Other sightings do not appear to correspond with this half form seen by Peter. In contrast, the ghost seen by a caretaker and on other occasions by cleaners, has been described as tall, willowy and wearing what appeared to be the dress of the Norman period.

WITNEY GHOST EVENT 2

WINES AND A SPIRIT

Two well known and much loved old Witonians, have between them, provided me with the following stories which I have included in the Witney 'Ghost Walk'. My grateful thanks are therefore due to these two pillars of the establishment, Ken Cook and Tom Worley. Kempster's music store once stood on the spot now occupied by Unwin's wine store, where Ken Cook was the manager of this once thriving establishment and spent most of his working life there.

Prior to Jack Kempster taking over the premises in 1930, the Gas, Coal and Coke Co occupied the building, and their manager, Mr Luckin, committed suicide by hanging himself in the living quarters situated over the shop.Ken was only vaguely aware of the dreadful tragedy which had occurred and did not overly concern himself with what had happened to the Gas, Coal & Coke Company's manager, until he began to hear footsteps and feel, 'a presence'. Strange noises would emanate from the first floor rooms and footsteps could be heard going down the stairs, this was despite the fact that Ken was the only person present. On one occasion a colleague returned from an upstairs room, asked who else was living there as he had heard someone moving about on the first floor, followed by footsteps rapidly descending the stairs. This colleague had absolutely no inkling of the tragedy, or of the other weird happenings within the house.

Ken became so fed up with the ghostly presence, that he finally rid himself of it by the simple expedient of standing at the bottom of the stairs and loudly asking Mr Luckin to kindly leave the premises. Ken was never again personally troubled by the ghostly noises, but other people visiting and living on the premises during the ensuing years, still heard the strange sounds and phantom footsteps. David Parsons, the present occupier of the premises, related this strange little tale to me. Apparently Hannah, David's teenage daughter was alone in her bed-room listening to music. She was intrigued to hear someone call her name several times and thinking it was her father in the next room, she made her way to where David was and asked him what he wanted. Her father was bewildered and remarked that it was a wonder she could hear anything above the din in her room, and no he had not called her. A voice from the past perhaps, or a spirit not contained within a bottle in the wine store?

Ken also relates a tale which is remarkable for the similarity to other visitations from the nearest and dearest who have passed to the other side. Having received a phone call from a Mr Monty Prior of Kidlington, regarding the disposal of a piano, Ken visited Mr Prior at his home. It appeared that the gentleman's wife had just recently died and as she had been the only person interested in the piano, he had decided to sell the instrument. The piano was duly inspected and both Ken and Mr Prior retired to the kitchen to discuss terms. During the conversation Mr Prior made one or two derogatory remarks regarding his late lamented wife while the two men were facing each other in the kitchen, Ken standing with his back to the kitchen door facing the sink and draining board. Mr Prior was facing the door, with his back to the sink. Finally a sum acceptable to both parties was agreed and a deal struck. The two men were just shaking hands on it when Mr Prior stated that his wife would have been pleased with the swift way negotiations had gone, as she had always been impatient and had the temperament of a sergeant major! No sooner had he uttered the words when a large plastic washing up bowl levitated from the draining board, travelled to the centre of the kitchen and there smashed onto the floor.Obviously the late Mrs Prior was not too enamoured of the way her husband had been speaking about her and had expressed her displeasure by picking up the bowl and throwing it at her husband. Needless to say Ken brought matters to a swift conclusion and hurriedly departed.

GHOST EVENT 3

HORROR AT THE WITNEY WHITE HART

The year 1652 witnessed Witney's worst loss of life in any one time and place, that place being the old White Hart then situated in Mill Street. The White Hart, at that time, was Witney's premier hostelry, catering to the carriage trade which passed through the town, on what was then the major route to Cheltenham and Wales. It was a well used staging post and extremely popular with both locals and travellers alike. The events leading up to the tragedy started when mummers, most of whom came from Stanton Harcourt, attempted to hire the town hall, or other public building of similar size, in which to present their play. However, both church and civic authorities considered the entertainment unsuitable for public consumption and thus refused permission. The mummers, not to be outdone, decided to hire the old White Hart, it then being the largest establishment in the locality, after the public buildings in Witney. This they did and the first performance commenced at seven in the evening. The play had been running for just over an hour when the floor of the upstairs room, in which the performance was taking place, began to give way. It must have been an horrific scene as the floor slowly disintegrated beneath the feet of both audience and players; there was no escape as the floor, players and the packed audience crashed down into the room below, killing some and injuring many. Five of Witney's townsfolk died that night and a further sixty were injured, some seriously, women and children as well as their menfolk were among the dead and injured, while the sounds of suffering from that disastrous night must have been heart rending, as a Witney elder stated at the time, "For some time after the event, a wailing and a weeping as if from Hell, arose from that accursed spot.'

The old White Hart was situated in Mill Street almost opposite what is now Wesley Barrell. At the time of the disaster, the White Hart brewery was joined onto the inn and it is understood that a

Old White Hart

Witney in the early 1960's. Where the old 'White Hart' once stood in Bridge Street.
Photograph by kind permission of Witney and District Historical Society.

family called Yates owned the whole structure, which contained both brewery and hostelry. The horrific accident occurred on 3 February 1652, and the heart rending cries of young children and the wails of their parents have been heard during the night of the 3rd and 4th of February on many occasions down through the years. Here are two reports of what appears to be a spirit world re-enactment of what took place on that fateful night almost three hundred years ago. In eighteen twenty three, John Hudson, a visitor from Gloucester, was approaching the site of the White Hart, when he observed what he took to be, 'A terrible accident unfolding before my very eyes, there were loud cries for help, children's screams and the whole of the roadway was smothered in dust'.

'I was not more than one hundred and fifty yards from this awful sight and the remarkable thing is that as I got nearer, the whole wondrous vision vanished before my very eyes'.

Another report tells a very similar story, but this time two locals from Witney apparently observed a number of men scrambling out of a building and falling into the road, again the vision appears to have been accompanied with cries and screams. As recently as the 1980's, there have been cries of distress heard, coming from what was once the White Hart, and the year 2002 will see the three hundred and fiftieth anniversary of this tragic event.

GHOST EVENT 4

DEATH ON THE BRIDGE

A religious procession marking the end of Easter and the resurrection was at one time a great annual event in Witney, but this eleventh century celebration slowly deteriorated from a well ordered Christian affair organised by the church into a commercial opportunity seized upon by cheapjacks, pedlars and tinkers, making it the perfect excuse for heavy drinking by the locals of Witney and its surrounding parishes. The original procession organised and marshalled by priests, had puppets representing several biblical characters, which were apparently manipulated to great effect. One of the characters was named 'John, or Jack, Snacker of Witney'. He would strike two staves together making a continuous clacking noise, and this puppet's actions were later made into a toy, very popular with the young folk. The game even spread as far as London, and it is thought that John or Jack represented the watchman at Christ's tomb, who upon seeing Christ arising, alerted the populace with the banging together of two sticks.

Following the influx of pedlars, cheapjacks etc, the feast day became an excuse for drunkenness and debauchery, while the religious significance became secondary to the money-making opportunities the day provided. Strong drink, bogus religious relics, trinkets and trivia became the order of the day so the church decided that the significance of the day had been lost to the irreligious mob, abandoned the day as a feast day and forbade any further processions.Local folklore holds, that the bridge crossing the river Windrush at the junction of Bridge Street and High Street, played an important role in the procession with blessings performed as flowers were floated into the waters of the river. The structure now spanning the river has evolved from a simple Saxon stepping stone crossing, into what is now an extremely busy route through Witney. The significance of the bridge in the annual procession was not lost upon the mob. On the final feast night and armed with whatever implements were to hand, a drunken crowd made their way to the bridge which they intended to destroy unless the church edict forbidding the procession, was withdrawn. Legend has it that a young novice priest was attempting to reason with the mob, when in a drunken fury the ringleaders, hurled him off the bridge, whereupon the young man fell to his death in the waters of the Windrush.

The legend of that day remains with us that, on the anniversary of the procession at Easter time, the poor young novice can be seen floating face down in the waters of the Windrush passing beneath the bridge. The young novice has been sighted on many occasions down through the centuries, but there are

The bridge over the Windrush at Witney, site of the events detailed in 'Death on the bridge' account.

no reports of him having been seen in recent years. Perhaps he has taken his last dip, or if anyone has spotted anything unusual in that part of the Windrush, they probably mistook it for yet another supermarket trolley ! The reported sightings have all taken place after 8 pm on the third day after Easter and it would seem that the best sightings occur between eleven and midnight on the anniversary of the tragic event. Walking towards Staple Hall from the town, cross to the right hand side of the bridge, look toward the left hand span, and who knows, you may, with any luck and a clear sky, see again the shade of the pious young man floating slowly down stream beneath the bridge.

GHOST EVENT 5

THE STUDENTS OF STAPLE HALL

It is believed that the building known as Staple Hall, built during the fourteenth century, then to all intents and purposes, totally rebuilt in the seventeenth following a fire, was used as a place of refuge from the plague, which struck periodically in Oxfordshire. During the sixteenth century Sir Thomas Pope of Trinity College Oxford, would send both fellows and students of Trinity college out into the country, taking them away from the heavily populated and hence plague vulnerable areas around Oxford. Both Witney and Garsington were areas he selected. Staple Hall, now a nursing

home, stands opposite the West End turn off and gives its name to
that location. In its heyday the Hall was one of the premier inns in
Witney, catering to the coaching trade on the route from London to
Cheltenham and westward.

THE LADY OF THE BLUE ROOM

Staple Hall is also home to the spirit of a very beautiful young lady
who haunts the first floor of this grand old residence. The young
woman, dressed in a long ball gown and sporting a diamond
necklace, strolls elegantly into what used to be the blue room
situated on the first floor. In the mid nineteen forties, week-end
guests of the then resident, the Registrar of Witney, used to play at
ghost spotting. Many of these visitors reported the sound of
footsteps rapidly approaching then stopping outside one particular
bedroom door, this was the door of the original 'blue-room', which
originally functioned as 'withdrawing room', to which diners would
retire following dinner.

One such visitor, Mr Ken Cook of Witney, spent an eventful
weekend at the Hall. Ken tells of how a sudden chill penetrated the
bedroom in which he was lodged. This was immediately followed
by the sound of a woman's footsteps walking along the passage-
way. They stopped immediately outside his door. Ken, his curiosity
aroused, immediately opened the bedroom door, but there was not
a soul in sight. Needless to say it was the first and the last time he
was an overnight visitor to Staples Hall.

GHOST EVENT 6

THE JOLLY TUCKER

The Jolly Tucker, which takes its name from one of the many trades
associated with the blanket industry which once flourished in the
area, once stood in the West End, where the Post Office now
stands. More an ale-house than an inn, this small pub used to
serve the local community rather than travellers, and was a
favourite place of the Tuckers who were responsible for 'fulling and
tentering' the blanket material. There is a very old song entitled
'The Jolly Tucker' and this would be performed annually at The
Tuckers' Feast. During the 20th, century, Jack Tooley was probably
the most noted performer of this song. Hopefully this old custom
will still linger on, although with the death of Richard Early during

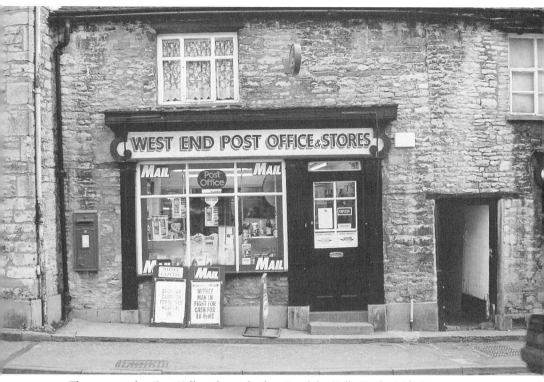

The present day Post Office, formerly the site of the 'Jolly Tucker' Ale House in West End, Witney.

1977, aged 88, the custom appears to have been largely forgotten. Fred Quatermain, well known ladies' hairdresser who used to run a salon in West End, once reported seeing the ghost of a young woman on the stairs leading to the upper rooms of the pub. This was, apparently, not an unusual event. In fact one landlady who had charge of the establishment in 1940, would hold regular one way conversations with the feminine apparition as they passed on the stairs. The ghost is believed to be that of a previous landlord's wife who had met her death in the ale house during the 19th century. I and my fellow researchers are unaware of there being any ongoing problems at the site where the Jolly Tucker once stood and upon which the Post Office now stands. However, Post Office customers should be aware that the apparition only haunts from half way up the stairs, to the landing!

Also in West End, stands number forty eight. This is the house which inspired a smash hit song of the First World War, you might say it has a haunting melody! The song was entitled 'The Old Fashioned Town'. Words and music were by Ada Leanora Harris and the inspiration for the song came from her Uncle and Aunt's 'old fashioned house in that old fashioned street', with Mr and Mrs Harris being 'that old fashioned pair'. Another famous person who was born and brought up in West End was Dr. Patrick Steptoe, pioneer of artificial insemination.

GHOST EVENT 7

THE SPECTRE OF PARLIAMENT HOUSE

In Corn Street, on the corner of the Crofts, the lovely old dwelling once known as 'Parliament House' stands, and there are two possible sources for this evocative name. In J.A. Giles' 'History of Witney', it is suggested that Witney is derived from the Anglo-Saxon names of, Witan-ige or Witan-eye, which meant 'Island of the Parliament'. The 'Book of Oxfordshire Place Names', by Margaret Gelling, advises us that Witney is derived from Wittas Island,being 'The Water Meadow of Witta', Witta being a local chieftain. It has also been suggested that James the First held a Parliament here in Witney, and the venue wherein this supposed Parliament was held, would naturally enough, have taken the name 'Parliament House'.

From whatever source the old building received its name, we could probably argue about until Doomsday, however, what we do know for certain is that 'Parliament House' is haunted by the ghost of a young servant girl.

The description given of her is as follows:

She has the appearance of a young woman of between eighteen and twenty years of age, with dark hair, dark eyes and a good complexion. She appears to be some five feet four inches tall, which was tall for her day; all in all an extremely attractive young lady. The clothes she is wearing would be a typical nineteen twenties 'between stairs' uniform as worn by a maid-servant, consisting of a black dress, starched white apron and a white cap covering the front of her head, apparently she looks for all the world as though she had just stepped out of the 'Upstairs Downstairs', television series.

The ghost, spectre or whatever the apparition may be, appears in 'solid' form, giving the impression of being as solid as you or I. It is more usual for an apparition of this kind to be at least semi transparent or wraith like, but the maid appears as a fully paid up member of the earthly human race.

To further enhance the earthliness of the apparition, she once appeared at the bedside of a tenant in the house. He was fast asleep at six fifteen on the morning of December third, when he heard a knock upon his bedroom door, and thinking it was one of his children messing about he called out 'come in and have a thrashing'. He was amazed when this 'housemaid', duly walked in carrying a tray on which there was a tea-pot, sugar bowl, cup, saucer and milk jug, all apparently in stirling silver. The 'maid' placed the tray upon his bed-side table, curtsied and walked out of the room. What however was truly amazing was that the 'maid' had apparently knocked, physically opened the door, deposited the tray, then left the bed-room closing the door behind her, whereupon the tray and its burden promptly vanished into thin air.

Exhaustive enquiries failed to explain what had happened on that cold December morning, but the tenant was relieved to learn that he was not alone in having witnessed this curious phenomenon. The then owner was apparently well acquainted with the 'young maid', and she had 'waited' upon his family for a number of years.

During the 1950's, a strange discovery was made by a well known local tradesman, Tom Smith of Newland, whilst he was working at Parliament House. Tom, together with one of his tradesmen, was carrying out renovation work, during which they discovered a walled-up room. The discovery was not commented upon by the owner, and no attempt was made to open the secret room, which remained sealed until the summer of 1995, when, Darrel Henly and Jeff Ricketts, were contracted to carry out renovation work for the Abbeyfield Soc., which had recently taken over the premises. Both Darrel and Jeff became aware that something was not right when they came to install plumbed facilities within some rooms; the introduction of new wiring and power points revealed further anomalies. Following measurements taken both from the outside and interior of the premises they concluded that there had to be a room or rooms concealed within the upper storey of the house. Following an intensive search, a hidden staircase was discovered, which was found to lead to an upstairs room which had been walled up many years previously. When they eventually opened the room, there was nothing to indicate either why it had been walled up, or when. What purpose this secret room had served has never been discovered and it is not for us to speculate here. However, when a spirit is earth bound, it usually indicates that some traumatic experience has occurred during the mortal life of the spirit, which anchors it to the earth. It seems an odd coincidence that a ghostly maid, and such a fair one, should be associated with a house containing a secret and walled up room ! The permutations of such a set of circumstances give almost endless scope for the imagination.

GHOST EVENT 7

THE ANGEL'S CURSE

This tale was recounted to the author by a much respected and regular patron of the establishment wherein this story of intrigue and violence took place. The Angel Inn is situated in Market Square, and is noted for its good food, fine ales and warm welcoming atmosphere, the ideal place wherein to rest your limbs following the completion of the 'Ghost Walk'.

The period in which this story unfolds is the early nineteenth century and it was related to me by a local person, the last surviving relative of the hero, some would say villain, of the tale. Within the Angel Inn, that most welcoming of Witney hostelries, there once stood an old wooden high stool, which was placed at the end of the bar, as far as possible from the public. Access to the stool was not easy, although it had the appearance of being an ordinary everyday type of stool, it was not. 'The Stool', was cursed. So potent was this curse, that the stool was removed from the bar in eighteen forty seven, and now the whereabouts of the cursed item is known only to one man, who is in fact the sole surviving member of the family from whence the curse sprang. It now appears certain that all trace of the cursed seat will disappear when Kenneth, the last of the line of Albert, the central character in the tale, dies. As one regular at the Angel said, "I trust the old bugger will burn the thing afore he snuffs it". For the sake of the peace of mind of many locals, it is to be hoped that 'the thing' will be destroyed well prior to Kenneth's death. Here then is the story of Albert's curse.

Albert was a married man who dwelled in Corn Street, Witney. This young man was well known in the town for his amorous advances to anyone, and it has been said, everyone female, married or unmarried it mattered not to Albert. He would pursue, what he perceived to be his quarry, relentlessly, until he had achieved his wicked way. Albert's latest, and it was to prove final conquest, was the wife of a local dignitary, the owner of a clothing emporium, who was also a lay preacher and graphic depictor of what hell was like for those who strayed or fell by the wayside. Fire, brimstone and a very large shovel appeared to be the basic elements awaiting all sinners.

The tread of heavy footsteps mounting the stairs which led to bedrooms of the clothier's home, alerted Albert to the fact that he and his latest conquest were no longer alone, the husband had returned home much earlier than expected, and he was now approaching the bedroom in which the amorous Albert and the husband's wife lay. Without a moment's hesitation Albert launched himself through the bedroom window which, fortunately for Albert, was conveniently open, but unfortunately for Albert also happened to be two floors up. Albert landed in a freshly deposited, very large, very smelly heap of manure, destined to be spread upon the adjacent fields

The Angel Inn on Church Green, Witney, Bedecked with summer flowers.

the very next day. The soft heap of evil smelling manure broke Albert's fall, and suffering no more than a twisted ankle and a hint of damaged pride he staggered off to The Angel, covered from head to toe in manure and stinking to high heaven.

The enraged husband had by now worked out what had been occurring in his absence and set off in hot pursuit of his quarry, a task greatly simplified by the stinking trail left by the amorous Albert, so that the husband simply followed his nose which led him directly to The Angel. There sat Albert, attempting to look as innocent as possible, but sitting on 'The Stool' at the corner of the bar covered in the evil smelling substance he stuck out like a sore

Outside view of the Angel Inn, market square. For many years, the place where the cursed stool resided.

thumb. The, by now totally enraged husband, readily identified Albert as his quarry and fetched him an enormous blow to the body, which lifted Albert, 'The Stool', a large quantity of glasses and the eyebrows of the patrons by several inches. Albert, by then firmly attached to 'The Stool', by several layers of rapidly drying manure, fell backwards fetching his head a sharp crack on the corner of the highly polished bar. This was a fatal blow, and as Albert lay dying on the bar-room floor cradled in the arms of the Landlord, he managed to summon up sufficient strength to place a curse upon 'The Stool', and anyone who sat thereon. A close friend of the stricken man, a local poet and heavy drinker, then composed a warning in rhyme foretelling the fate of anyone foolish enough to sit on the cursed stool.

The Cursed Stool
Look close upon this cursed stool
And you will see
The deep dark stain that
Once were me
For I were killed
Afore my time
My manhood cut whilst in its prime
So cursed be them
Who'd sit upon this stool
Be they wise-man or be they fool
And this is how the curse will be
Layed out here for all to see
'As in a dream your fate you'll see
Then death will follow on day three'

And so 'The Angel's' curse was cast. Albert was buried. The lay preacher divorced. His wife married the gardener. Albert's family were placed in the 'Wuk-uss' and four people died in various dramatic circumstances either while sitting on or soon after rising from 'The Stool'.

THE BURWELL VISITOR
I can offer no explanation for the following strange, but absolutely true, occurrences which take place within the home of a perfectly normal couple living on the Burwell Farm estate to the west of Witney. The lady of the house, married for some twenty years, became aware of a presence standing at the side of her bed, she did not feel threatened in any way and believed that she had been dreaming and had carried the dream through to her waking moments. The following night she again became aware of the figure standing in the same spot that it had occupied the previous night. She describes the figure as a male about five feet in height, fair hair cut short and brushed forward, delicate features, blue eyes and a large forehead.

There was a tranquillity about the figure which seemed to fill the bedroom and a benignity which pervaded her mind. She described it as an almost holy experience, the figure stood looking at her for about two minutes then slowly disappeared.

A local woman who is a friend of the family and is also a gifted psychic has agreed to investigate and attempt to achieve an

explanation for this phenomenon, meanwhile the figure is still a
regular visitor to the house.

ALBERT TOOLEY AND THE HEADLESS HORSEMAN

A well known and likeable character, Albert Tooley, who resided in
Witney, never tired of recounting this next tale, and though the
passage of time has dimmed the exact location and circumstances
surrounding the events, in essence the story is true.

It appears that Albert was returning from a night out at a local
hostelry where he had, as Albert put it, 'Imbibed freely but not
wantonly!', the time was approximately eleven p.m. and it was a
bright, frosty night in December. He heard the sound of a horse and
carriage approaching him from behind, which alerted Albert to the
fact that he was not alone on that lonely stretch of road running
from Hailey into Witney, but it seemed exceedingly peculiar that a
horse and carriage should be on the road at that time of night.
Albert, who was on his push bike, ceased pedalling, placed one
foot on the ground and turned to face the oncoming vehicle, when
the hairs on the back of Albert's neck stood straight on end. It was
as though he had been struck by lightning as the nervous shock of
what he was observing hit him. There seated on a four wheeled cart
and pulled by an enormous black horse sat a headless man,
dressed in a huge old army greatcoat, holding a whip and driving
straight towards Albert. Without pause the bicycle went one way
and Albert went the other, the bicycle ending up in the road and
Albert in the ditch, and from his vantage point in the ditch Albert
watched as the whole hideous spectacle bore down upon him. He
was not aware of there being anything abnormal or supernatural
stalking the Hailey to Witney road, and as he explained later, he
had met a few mindless people on that stretch of road, but never a
headless one.Numerous thoughts ran through Albert's mind as he
peered from the ditch, "Could this be part of a television
programme? was it a practical joke ?" But there was not another
soul to be seen only the clip clop of the hooves and the rumble of
the cart wheels as the ghostly apparition drew ever nearer.

The headless horror was now within a few yards of where Albert
lay and it was drawing to a halt. "My God" he thought, "That's it,
I'm done for." The cart, the huge black horse and the headless
driver were now no more than five yards from where Albert lay, 'Is
that you Albert?' a voice queried from inside the voluminous army
great coat, "What do you want, is it my time?" Albert responded.
"Oh it's about eleven o'clock and I'm just moving a few things from

the farm to my daughter's new house, she's moving in tomorrow",
the greatcoat replied, "it's bloody cold isn't it, I forgot the old
balaclava and my bloody ears are frozen." All this was being said
whilst the head of one of Albert's many acquaintances emerged
from inside the greatcoat. "Yes it is bloody cold, must get on,"
Albert replied, as he scrambled from the ditch and picked up his
bicycle, "Must get this bloody thing fixed, the chain keeps coming
of and throwing me, see you tomorrow Tom," and off he went,
pushing his bike, bruised, battered but tremendously relieved not
to have been overtaken by the unknown, and thankful that he had
retained his dignity throughout, or so he thought. Needless to say
the frightful story spread and whilst the laugh may have been on
Albert, the pints were on other people when he was requested to
relate the tale of the 'Headless Horseman'!

THE PHOTOGRAPH

A strange tale of the supernatural concerning a marriage break-up,
a nine year old boy and an amazing photograph was related to me
by the boy's grandmother. In a village situated only two miles from
Witney, the name of which is witheld out of respect for the feelings
of the family, but a village noted for its success in the world of
horticulture, lived a family who were staunch supporters of the
local horticultural society. They had for many years entered into
the annual show, some exceedingly good plant specimens.
However no matter how excellent their exhibits, the family had
never succeeded in claiming a first prize in any classification. It
had become a standing joke in the village that, if they entered the
best bloom in the world someone else would pip them by entering
the best bloom in the universe, nevertheless their commitment was
total and come what may, the family never failed to enter into the
spirit of all true amateur events, 'Its not the winning but how you
play the game.'

The young boy's parents were experiencing difficulties in their
marriage and divorce appeared to be well and truly on the cards.
Donald, the young son was bewildered and not a little bit afraid of
what he perceived to be constant rows and screaming matches
between his parents; one severe argument had ended up with the
police intervening following an assault upon his wife by the
enraged husband. The one refuge that Donald could turn to when
life became unbearable for him was the garden. He had inherited
his forebears love of horticulture and had his own patch of garden,
which together with the shed, secluded behind a row of laurels,

was his haven of peace. His grandmother was also a tower of strength to the bewildered young boy and she would whenever possible, provide comfort and some security for him.

The first intimation that anything out of the ordinary was happening to Donald was when on one of his grandmother's visits, he informed her that he had 'A new friend who was going to help him win this years top award in the annual show'. Don's grandmother was pleased that the boy was happier than she had seen him since his parent's break-up and she asked who his new friend was. "Well, I'm not supposed to tell anyone, but I don't think he will mind you knowing. His name's Adam and he's a gardener". "Where do you see him", Don's grandmother queried. "He comes round the garden, then we sit in the shed and he tells me about all the times he tried to win the horticultural competition but he always came second too. This year, with Adam's help our family will take first prize and then perhaps Mum and Dad will get back together again". With that Don went back into the garden, with his grandmother tagging along behind. "Is Adam here now?" Gran asked, "Yes by the shed", Don replied, but gran could see no one. Not wishing to make an issue of the situation and assuming that Don had invented an imaginary friend, grandmother kept silent until her daughter, Don's mother, mentioned that she was concerned at the length of time Don was spending in the garden and of how she had seen him, more than once, speaking animatedly to someone who was completely invisible.

It was two days prior to the annual show when Don invited his grandmother to view his proposed entry, which he told his Gran, was the bloom that would take first prize, Adam had shown him how to tend it and he had also provided a special mixture which Don had to mix with water and sprinkle on the plant exactly two days prior to the day of the show. "This was the first sprinkling day", Don said excitedly, as they walked down the garden. Don and his grandmother walked to the bottom of the big garden then on into Don's small patch which was invisible from the house, it being screened by a privet hedge. Grandmother stopped and gazed in astonishment at what she took to be 'the bloom'; it was the most perfect flower she had ever seen. It came as an even greater surprise to her as everyone had been barred from Don's garden, apparently upon the mysterious Adam's orders, until the two friends agreed 'the bloom', was ready for the show.

It was the night before the show and to Don it was probably the happiest night of his life because his father, mother and grandmother were all accompanying him on the following day. "I suppose your friend Adam's coming too?" teased his mother, "Yes he will be there", Don replied. Don's father was aware of the friendship his son had struck up with the invisible, mysterious Adam; he had also been made acutely aware of the misery the whole family had gone through since the marriage break-up. His son's apparent adoption of a phantom father figure in Adam, had brought home just how much he missed his family. His wife had informed him that Adam had told Don the family would be back together again immediately after the show. It was the day of the show and time for the presentation of prizes. Don's beautiful bloom had been duly awarded 'top show specimen', Don with his whole family was up on stage, Don to receive his presentation and the family to receive a special commendation for their years of service to the society. Don proudly stood between his grandmother, father and mother to have photographs taken for the local newspaper, the cup was lifted aloft and the family grinning broadly were photographed holding the 'top show specimen'.

It was four days following the show that the local newspapers published the results along with photographs of the prize winners. Don's mother had picked up three copies from the local newsagents and hurried home to read what had been said about her son, and also of course, to view the photographs. Her mother was waiting for her and they both entered the house where Don was sitting quietly reading a book. Mother and daughter opened their papers almost simultaneously and both looked at each other unbelievingly, after gazing at the photograph in the newspaper, for there standing behind Don with his hands resting lightly on the boy's shoulders stood his grandfather, a grandfather who had been dead for seventeen years. "Is this Adam standing behind you in the photographs?", his mother asked Don. "Yes, that's him, I told you he would be there, he said he'd waited almost twenty years to win that prize and he wouldn't miss it for the world."

The photograph of four people and a phantom takes pride of place on the mantle shelf of an old lady who lives in Witney; her daughter has a copy of that same photograph hanging in the bedroom of her home in Woodstock.

Don has a young family of his own now and I asked him if he had told his young daughter of the events leading to that incredible photograph. He explained that his daughter was not as yet old enough to understand, but when she was, he would take her back and step by step make her aware of the circumstances surrounding the last visit of her great-grandfather.

THE SPINNERS REVENGE

'New Mills', or as it is now known locally, 'Newmill', is popularly considered to be the first woollen mill established on the banks of the River Windrush; it also holds the distinction of being one of the first mills in Witney to be mechanised.

Prior to the arrival of mechanisation, all local spinning was done by hand. During the latter years of the eighteenth century Edmund Wright, introduced new mechanised techniques for spinning wool, which enabled the mill owners to produce greater quantities of cloth from the use of a much reduced staff. This was a massive blow to the local spinners who immediately found themselves not just unemployed, but destitute. Nevertheless, despite severe antagonism from and great suffering among the erstwhile workers, the new technology was put into use, driven by economic necessity and not a little greed, while the workers suffered in poverty.

It is generally believed, but has never been conclusively proven, that Witney spinners, on several occasions, attempted to burn down Newmill, the focus of their misery. What is known, is that the mill was severely damaged by fire on no less than three occasions, with the main buildings having to be almost completely re-built in the eighteen eighties.

It appears however, that fate had already played a hand in the spinners' revenge at a much earlier date. During the seventeen nineties Edmund Wright, the man responsible for the introduction of the mechanised system, mysteriously plunged to his death in the mill pond. Accident or not, the redundant spinners were delighted that the man they considered responsible for their dire circumstances, had met his death beneath the very water wheel he had recently installed to drive the mill machinery which had so cruelly robbed them of their livelihoods.

Several months after the death and burial of Edmund Wright, his body was seen floating below the surface of the waters near the mill. A subsequent investigation established that the figure sighted could not possibly have been that of Edmund Wright, as he was still safely at rest and his grave was undisturbed. But, Edmund would not go away and was seen again and again, hovering by or just beneath the surface of the mill-pond.

Since those first sightings, the ghost of Edmund Wright has been a regular inhabitant of the mill. Could it be that he repents in death, the misery he caused to so many of his fellow human beings, or if he was pushed to his death, does he return in the hope of pointing the finger at his murderer? What he may think of the modern technology which he encounters during his visits to Newmill, is anyone's guess! It seems reasonable to assume that he would be unhappy that the machinery he introduced which once spun the wool that made the famous Witney blankets is no more, but as an innovator himself, he will no doubt accept the march of progress as inevitable. Among the old mill workers are still many who recount tales of having seen the lonely figure of poor Edmund as he still haunts what was once the oldest blanket makers in Witney.

Newmill still stands in Witney and ironically, houses a modern high technology development company. Edmund would no doubt find this an acceptable use for his property.

One of the New Mill sluices on the river Windrush at Witney.

CHAPTER THREE

SUPERNATURAL EVENTS IN:
HANBOROUGH AND WOODSTOCK

The Ghostly Monk

The five monks filed past Mary's cottage window, heads bowed deep in prayer as they made their way to the hospital recently set within the grounds of the monastery, which had been opened to accommodate victims of the plague; it was one of the few places wherein some comfort from the pain and degradation of that dreadful sickness could be found. As the five cowled figures slowly passed the cottage the monk bringing up the rear of the party raised his head and smiled at Mary, she in turn smiled back at him, then followed with her eyes the five figures until they disappeared from her view.

Mary then moved back into her tiny living room stirring the fire until a cheerful blaze ensued. Mounting the stairs situated in the corner of the room, she made her way to a back bedroom. Once there, she took out from under a loose floor board a delicately carved wooden box and emptied the contents onto her bed cover. Out tumbled a small silver crucifix, a silken ribbon and a cascade of silver coins. Mary carefully checked the amount which had a total value of two hundred and ten pounds, a fortune in those days, the year being sixteen eighty. This was Mary's insurance against rapidly approaching old age, her late husband and his father had accumulated this money through hard years of bone aching hours of toil. She had seen both of them die of the plague only eighteen months previously and this was when she had made the acquaintance of Brother Thomas, one of the monks tending the plague victims.

Brother Thomas was not the kind of monk the brothers within the monastery were used to, having travelled from no one knew where, to arrive one late December day begging permission to remain and become a novice. Due to the many plague victims being tended by the brothers, he was accepted immediately, an extra pair of hands was surely a gift from God. Brother Thomas was small wiry and ungodly, with his nut brown face and merry eyes he appeared more like a tinker than a monk, however he quickly established himself in the village as a not unkindly man and definitely not a holy one, he had far too great a fondness for the local brew and the maids of Hanborough.

Brother Thomas was in fact an outlaw, who had left the flesh pots of London for safer climes in the country, following his flight from justice after narrowly escaping arrest whilst breaking into a city merchant's home. Alas for all the piety and godliness within the order, Brother Thomas was not converted from his wicked ways, soon being aware of his next victim whose confidence he had already won. He intended to steal from Mary, having learned of her riches whilst attending her plague stricken husband.

It was late October in the early hours of a Monday morning when Mary was awakened by the sound of a door closing. She climbed from her bed and walked through the house checking doors and windows, finding nothing amiss she returned to her bedroom, moved to the window and resting her head in her hands peered down the garden. To her surprise, she spotted a small wiry figure with brown robes hitched up around its waist, scurrying rapidly down the garden path. Mary's heart lurched as she moved swiftly to retrieve the precious box concealed beneath the floor board, but it had gone. A search of the house confirmed poor Mary's worst fears, the much trusted Brother Thomas had stolen her savings and she was now destitute.

It came as no surprise to the Brothers or the villagers, to find that Brother Thomas had disappeared along with Mary's box. Following the loss of her few treasured possessions along with the money, Mary went into a rapid decline, her last few remaining weeks were spent in repeatedly searching the cottage, but her searches were always fruitless and within three months Mary had wasted away and was dead.

Over two hundred years on Mary still searches for her stolen treasure and she will continue to do so for as long as her cottage stands in Long Hanborough. Janet and Gerry of Millwood End can vouch for this as explained in the next tale of the supernatural.

THE HANBOROUGH HAUNTINGS

Mary of Millwood End

The cottage, nestling in a row of five similar properties, had nothing to distinguish it from its neighbours, each having neat well-tended gardens overlooking a little used road, which once led to the monastery and hospital, wherein the monks tended to victims of the plague. Mellow yellow Cotswold stone flanked the strong oak front door, the walk up the garden path to the front door was a short one, the paving showing wear and tear of over two hundred years constant use.

The door opened to my knock and I was instantly taken back 200 years. The current owners, Janet and Gerald Webb, have restored the cottage to its original appearance, being that of a farm worker's cottage. Certainly some minor alterations had been made, but the original stonework, fireplaces, beams etc., had been lovingly and painstakingly restored.

The Webbs have been living at the cottage for the past twenty years, having purchased it from Norman Shelley, the well-known actor and author, more famous perhaps for his voice-overs of Winston Churchill during the War years. These voice-overs were used to conceal the fact that Churchill was out of the country and hence to mislead German Intelligence regarding his whereabouts.

Stone set in the wall of the haunted cottage, the inscription is indecipherable.

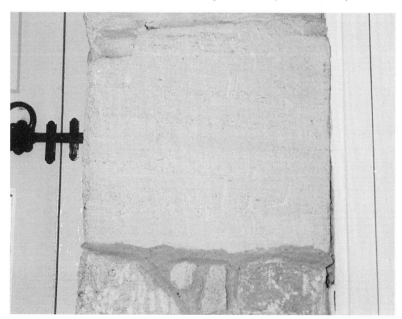

Norman Shelley had made no secret of the fact that the cottage was haunted, when selling to Gerald and Janet Webb, on the contrary, he had emphasised the presence of a ghost when concluding the deal. Gerald and Janet, both sceptics, did not let the possibility of a ghost, real or imagined, stand in the way of their dream home. Once over the threshold, they had both fallen in love with the house, even though its condition was less than perfect. The original Cotswold stone, inside what were to be the lounge and dining room areas, had been concreted over, beams hidden, fire places tiled over and a general attempt to conceal any original features had been initiated by several previous owners.

The first hint of what was to come occurred when Gerald was attempting to remove a mix of plaster and concrete from what was to become the lounge area walls. Every effort to remove this mix failed dismally, Gerald angrily informing Janet that he was going to knock the whole damned wall down, walked into the kitchen to drink a cup of tea. He took two sips, then walked back into the proposed lounge area, only to witness the plaster and concrete mix crumbling before his eyes. The couple were later to discover that the ghost did not like change, on this occasion it had chosen the lesser of two evils, rather than have a whole wall removed, it had allowed the disintegration of the concrete covering.

Once they were settled in, Janet began feeling the presence of something or someone in the cottage, not a frightening presence but definitely an uncomfortable one. This presence manifested itself in a number of ways, such as a change in temperature, a passing shadow, the sense of being brushed as though by a spider's web. Clearly far too many incidents for them to be regarded as accidental or within the normal range of unexplained events.

The first actual sighting came when Janet, was sitting in the lounge by the large brick fireplace. Suddenly sensing she was not alone, Janet looked up from the

The Fireplace where Janet first saw Ghost of old lady.

book she was reading and glanced toward the door leading into the kitchen. There, sitting in a narrow corner of the fireplace, sat a little old lady. Janet froze, her mind raced, attempting to find rational explanations: it was a shadow, it was smoke from the fire, it was, in fact, anything other than a ghost.

Speaking to Janet, you quickly discover that she is a level headed, sensible person who would rather there not be a ghost in her house. The apparition however, was real, no figment of her imagination, a tangible entity whose presence, after Janet's initial shock, looked perfectly at home sitting by the fire. "It felt", Janet said, "that she had as much right to be there as I had." This occurrence lasted for approximately three minutes. According to Janet, she was, in her words, too 'gobsmacked' to do anything except sit and stare at the apparition. She called Gerald, but the figure had already disappeared by the time he arrived. Gerald's comments were.

"You've been seeing things, there are no such things as ghosts. Better stay off the drink !."

Corner where old lady climbs no longer existing stairs.

Janet, however, knows that what she had seen was real.

Shortly after the fireplace incident came the mysterious brass incident. Janet had ten pieces of old brass, much loved and highly prized, which were taken down from the walls and regularly cleaned; this was Gerald's job. Gerald duly removed all ten brasses from the wall and proceeded to clean and polish them. Not

Ringed is the broken mushroom ornament.

pausing or stopping for anything, he finished each of the brasses then passed them to Janet for placing back on the wall. "Where's the owl?" asked Janet, "It's missing." "No, it's not", Gerald replied, "They are all there." "It's missing, it's my favourite and it's got to be found," was Janet's response. Both Janet and Gerald had not moved more than three or four yards from where they had been cleaning the brasses but despite turning the house upside down, the owl could not be found.

Three months after the disappearance of the brass, Janet had a bingo win and explained to Gerald that she was going to buy an owl to replace the missing one. Janet walked into the kitchen, put on her coat and walked back into the lounge to leave by the front door. Gerald had not moved from his position in the kitchen, but when Janet looked into the fireplace where she had spotted the old lady, there, highly polished and looking as good as new, lay her owl. Despite several unexplainable incidents, such as the disappearance and subsequent reappearance of the owl and the arrival of two relatives, both sceptics who said there were no such things as ghosts, they were all forced to change their minds when a light bulb shattered for no reason and the door of the grandmother clock sprang open. Other doors opened and shut of their own accord, footsteps were heard in the night, etc. Despite all this, Gerald was still sceptical about playing host to a ghost. That is until the early hours of a Friday morning, when he awoke with a start and observed a little old lady move down the side of the bedroom and take up a position at the bottom of the bed where she sat gazing out of the window head in hands, looking at the garden. There is no longer any doubt in Gerald's mind that there is a spirit, entity, ghost, call it what you will, residing in his home at Long Hanborough. In a strange twist to this tale I witnessed the following event....

Having finished the story, I returned to Gerald and Janet's together with Terry, my photographer, to take shots of the interior of the house; this was approximately four weeks after my first interview with them.

It was a beautiful summer day with brilliant sunshine, blue skies and that 'all's well with the world', feeling as we approached the cottage.

On the way to Hanborough from Witney, Terry, who had no knowledge of the events which had occurred in the cottage, had been voicing his opinion regarding the supernatural during our journey. Terry's opinion was much the same as the majority of other folks, sceptical but willing to be convinced. As we entered the cottage door he whispered, "I can't believe that anything or anyone would want to haunt or disturb a place so lovingly and painstakingly restored."

Janet had overheard this and she explained to Terry that the 'old lady', was quite harmless, even fun so long as she was informed of any changes that were about to take place within the cottage. As the photographs were being taken, Terry expressed the opinion that he hoped the 'old lady' had been told what was happening that day. It swiftly became apparent that Janet had forgotten to inform her 'old lady'. Following the completion of the photo-shoot, when all four of us were in the sitting room, the unmistakable sound of breaking china came from a room adjacent to the one in which we were sitting.

It took approximately four seconds for all of us to rush into the room from where the sound had come, where, taken from a set of three expensive porcelain mushrooms, which stood in a row upon a shelf measuring at least one foot wide and now lying shattered on the floor, was the middle mushroom; it must have travelled at least four feet before smashing. No human hand could possibly have caused the ornament to smash, there was no breeze and the width of the shelf precluded any possibility of the mushroom simply falling off. The distance from the shelf to where the object broke was four feet, no other person was present and no more than four seconds had elapsed from the time of the crash, to our arrival on the scene.

Terry is now a lot less sceptical regarding the supernatural and Janet, together with Gerald, never fails to have a word with their 'old lady', whenever change is envisaged or visitors expected.

HANBOROUGH HAUNTINGS

Old Mother Scalpepper of Hanborough.

In the mid sixteen hundreds, a Mrs Jane Colpepper came to a sticky end. There are a number of versions of how this came about, but the one which appears to have the most credence is that she was drowned in a large pool, which had been dug at the bottom of the rectory gardens. Whether poor Jane was murdered or whether her death was an accident, it seems that her spirit still haunts the scene of her death, despite exorcisms attempted by several clergymen. Old Mother Scalpepper, has been seen many times making her way from Church Hanborough to Eynsham along what was formerly a footpath between the two places. Perhaps she is nearing her time for departure from this mortal plane, as sightings of her are becoming progressively less frequent, particularly when you compare the frequency of sightings up until the 1930's, with the ever less frequent occurrences in recent years, suggesting Jane is rapidly fading away. Or could it be that her spirit is at last coming to terms with her untimely demise ?

Here is one reported sighting from two farm labourers, who were making their way home following a day in the fields. "We had a sight of an old lady, dressed very queerly on the path to Eynsham. She were tall and straight and she were moving slowly away from us. We didn't know who she were nor where she were from, so we hurried after her".

"It seemed strange that the more we tried to catch her up, the faster she managed to move away from us. We wish now that we hadn't bothered to try and catch up with her because just about half way along the path, she stopped, turned and started to walk back towards us. Her face were a terrible sight and she were dripping wet. We took to our heels and raced back the way we had come. That woman had only half a face and it looked for all the world as though she had just been dragged out of the river."

Jane is still about and, according to several locals, the best time to go 'Scalpepper spotting' is mid April in the evening. Apparently, it helps if you have a few at the Shepherd's Hall pub before you try your luck.

'Jericho Hall' The Hanborough Dandy

Another spirit who haunts the Hanborough area is 'Jericho Hall', who mostly frequents the Freeland road. He is described as being stockily built, wearing knee breeches, blue stockings, dark brown jerkin and fancy buckled shoes. Jericho was a fine wrestler and adept at 'knee kicking', stick fighting and fencing. He, in fact, used to organise all the foregoing pursuits in the area and was renowned as an instructor in these arts. Many dandies from London and the Shires were pupils of Jericho's and took part in his bi-annual contests, probably the forerunner of the sporting contests which used to take place at the annual 'Wychwood Fair'.

This is an account from Ken Bailey of Witney, who was returning by car to Witney from Bladon late one evening in October 1976.

"I was passing the Shepherd's Hall, just prior to the Freeland turn-off, when I spotted this figure in the oncoming lane. The figure appeared to have a glow surrounding it. I put my lights up to main beam, but there was absolutely no other vehicle in sight. I was however astonished to see this squat but extremely broad-shouldered man dressed in pantomime gear; that is, breeches, square toed silver buckled shoes, black loose fitting waistcoat over a floppy shirt. He looked for all the world like a figure from a regency play or film. He was also carrying a stick."

"I had slowed the car nearly to a standstill which was just as well because, as I got to the Freeland turn, the figure walked straight across the road directly in front of me. I stopped the car, opened my side window and peered out. I actually watched the figure slowly disappear before my eyes. First it was in full view just as I described it, then it became transparent, finally disappearing completely."

The Ghostly Monk

The following strange occurrences related to me by two sober and responsible citizens confirm reports of a phantom monk or monks, having been sighted in the Hanboroughs.

Mr John Lord of Hurdeswell, Long Hanborough, observed a figure dressed in what could have been the habit of a monk, passing the French doors at the rear of his house. This sighting occurred as John was dressing the Christmas tree on December 23rd 1997. The figure of a very tall man, grey in appearance and wearing a long voluminous coat or cloak passed before his eyes, travelling from right to left, the figure unhurriedly floated out of his field of vision to the left. John quickly switched off the lights and peered into the garden, but whatever it was, had simply floated through a six foot high solid brick wall.

Mr Alan Bennett of Coniston Avenue, Headington, observed the following as he drove through Church Hanborough into Lower Road. A tall figure wearing a hooded cloth coat or cloak was seen on the right hand side of the road, when without warning the figure stepped straight out into the road, forcing Alan to brake violently. The figure then floated diagonally across the road and simply disappeared into thin air. Two further tales of the supernatural from Hanborough, and if the reports continue to proliferate at this rate, this part of Oxfordshire will soon be in the Premier Division of haunted villages.

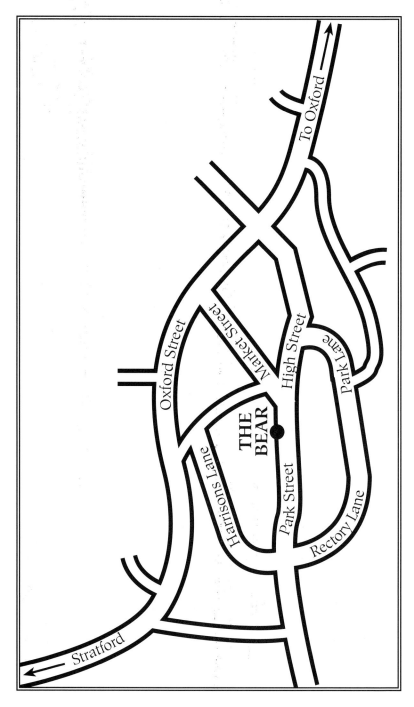

The location of 'The Bear' at Woodstock.

The Bear at Woodstock

'The Bear' hotel at Woodstock, is a name which dates back as far as the thirteenth century and in fact there has been an inn on the same site for well over eight hundred years. A listed building, 'The Bear' hotel has in recent years been tastefully and skilfully modernised, whilst retaining the essential character of this fine period building. The rich, the famous, the poor and the infamous have all left a little something of themselves within these ancient walls. The many travellers, together with the local people, have over the centuries, created an atmosphere unique to this wonderful and remarkable old inn.

Among others, Elizabeth Taylor, Richard Burton, Dick Turpin and a veritable who's who of the pop world have either stayed at or passed through 'The Bear', in fact it would be very surprising if someone internationally famous were not staying here on any given night. In keeping with the high standards and the ongoing history of this hotel, the staff are courteous, welcoming and helpful, while their fund of local knowledge make a stay at 'The Bear' an excellent jumping off point for those wishing to explore the area and its history. What is more, you also get a ghost thrown in at no extra cost.

Room sixteen at the hotel is a living reminder of the past, reached by a staircase dating back centuries, and was the scene of a sad and poignant event. An unmarried lady, rich, famous and one of the leading members of society, gave birth to a child in room sixteen; she and her maid were on their way to Scotland, where arrangements for the birth and the fostering of the illegitimate child had already been made. Unfortunately for all three, the baby was born prematurely and without medical help, a situation which led to the death almost immediately after its birth of the unfortunate mite. What with the shame, social stigma and stain upon the character of the family which would be heaped upon their good name if the story of her misfortune became known, the lady, with help from her maid servant, decided to conceal the body of the dead child in a recess below the bedroom windows, thus hopefully avoiding a terrible scandal.

Guests staying in room sixteen soon began complaining about the sounds of a child crying, despite assurances that there were no children staying in any adjoining room. The haunting sounds of a child in distress continued to bother some, but not all of the occupants of room sixteen. Shortly after the baby crying incidents, the ghostly figure of a young woman was seen, the phantom lady was not particularly associated with room sixteen, but she appeared to wander the corridors of the hotel immediately following the sound of childish crying, as if seeking its source.

In more recent times, the night porter at 'The Bear' experienced an incident which occurred at approximately three am, while he was on his usual night-time rounds which included checking fire doors. It was part of his job to ensure that each fire door opened and closed correctly. On this occasion however, each door he opened stubbornly refused to close no matter how often or how hard he slammed, and finally three of the doors just would not remain closed. The restaurant manager also witnessed these strange occurrences and he afterwards explained to the night porter that a lady had been following him as he went on his rounds and promptly opening the fire doors as swiftly as they were being closed. This same lady also awakened the manager's wife about one hour after the incidents with the doors. The manager's wife found herself rudely awakened by someone or something tugging at the bed clothes, she awoke with a start and watched as a short woman, with shorn hair and wearing a black dress which reached to the floor, angrily tried to pull the duvet off the bed.

Unsurprisingly, the manager's wife shrieked in fright, as a result of which the figure at the bottom of the bed promptly disappeared, whilst the manager himself was awakened by his wife's scream, but saw nothing. Young students from Oxford University deliberately booked into room sixteen with the aim of encountering the ghost, but had no luck with their mission. They did however say that during their stay the temperature in the room dropped at an alarming rate and remained icy cold for several minutes before returning to normal. This dropping of the temperature is a well known feature of room sixteen, and it is without question the coldest room in the hotel.

New members of staff at 'The Bear', chamber-maids in particular, are always given the task of preparing room sixteen for incoming guests. When their tasks are completed, they are always asked what they think of the room, and the reply is almost always the same, 'Its cold and has an atmosphere'. Well the room appears perfectly normal to me, it is in fact quite delightful and my stay there was entirely uneventful, however it is without doubt several degrees colder than any of the other rooms in the hotel.

CHAPTER FOUR

SUPERNATURAL EVENTS IN:
BRIZE NORTON

Louise and Billy looked bewildered and lost as they stood on the platform of Paddington station, clutching their mothers hands, they fitfully tugged at the string looped over their shoulders, moving the cardboard boxes containing their gas masks to a new position every few seconds. "Do stop twitching", Mum said, "it won't be long now and you'll be on the train and on the way to a safe place, well away from those German 'planes."

"I don't want to go", Billy cried. "Nor do I", chorused Louise. "You know its not safe in London with those bombers coming over every night and besides, what would your Dad say if he knew you were crying, he thinks you're brave little soldiers and it'll make it easier for him if he knows you're safe. Dad, was a sailor who would soon be serving on Russian convoy duty.

The platform was packed with children waiting to be evacuated from London, it was midway through the blitz and life was becoming unbearable. The almost nightly air raids had taken their toll and there was at that time a constant threat of being bombed out of your home, fear for the safety of the children at home and for loved ones in the armed services. It was a tremendous relief for parents to know that at least the children were being taken to a place of safety.

The train taking Billy and Louise from London was one of the last evacuee trains to leave the capital, bound for Oxfordshire where safe accommodation was awaiting those innocent victims of war.

A whistle blew, last waves were made and Billy with Louise settled into the seats in a carriage, packed with other evacuees. "Where is it we're going?", queried Billy, "Witney silly, how many times do I have to tell you?", replied Louise. Two hours later the train duly arrived at Witney station, where transport was waiting to take the children to their temporary homes.

Bill and Louise had been billeted with the Townsends who lived in Witney. Mr Townsend was in service in the Royal Navy, whilst his wife was working at one of the local blanket mills, as were so many of Witney's townsfolk. Billy and Louise quickly settled down to a routine, swiftly establishing themselves as part of the family. Witney was a far cry from their home amidst the hurly-burly of the East End of London, but it had its compensations, not least of which was watching the aircraft flying over from the nearby R.A.F. station at Brize Norton.

"One day we shall make a trip over to Brize Norton and let you see the aeroplanes actually take off", their teacher had promised. Billy excitedly discussed with Louise the prospect of going to see the aeroplanes, "Promise you won't go without me", Louise begged, Billy solemnly promised that if they couldn't go together then they shouldn't go at all. It took thirty years for Billy to fulfil his promise.

Chris's Tale

Chris Bromham had moved from his native Wales and settled in Brize Norton village and worked at the nearby Smiths Industries car heater factory. He was a down-to-earth practical man, with many friends both in the village and at his place of work.

Chris was not a person given to flights of fancy, almost the opposite in fact and this is the tale he recounted. If true, it is a most unusual story and I have no reason to believe otherwise, and the only explanation I can think of is a 'wish fulfilment', realised after thirty years. Because I cannot unearth any information as to why these two children should appear in such an unlikely place and at such an unlikely time, I have prefaced Chris Bromham's account with a fictitious 'stage setting' for the story.

"I felt as though I was dreaming, it was a Saturday afternoon in December, a slight drizzle was falling and it was beginning to turn dusk even though it was only four in the afternoon. The year was 1978 and I remember thinking there's a hell of a lot of activity from the airfield at Brize Norton, and it all seems to be old stuff, that is two and four piston engined aircraft, no jets at all.

As I walked from my house to the bus stop down the road I spotted two children standing on the opposite side of the approach road to Carterton. There were no adults except myself present, no traffic and there was an eerie silence and stillness about the place. I had never seen these two children before and they appeared to be either lost or waiting for someone. As I got nearer to them I could see that they were both wearing long grey raincoats and they were carrying what I immediately recognised as wartime gas masks in cardboard boxes. The children would have been no older than eight or nine years of age.

As I got to the two children they both looked straight up into my eyes and smiled, they held their hands out, which I took, and we all three crossed the road. The weirdest part of this whole thing was the fact that not one word was spoken yet I knew exactly what they required of me. As we got to the other side of the road the children simultaneously let go of my hands and started to walk off. They had travelled about fifteen to twenty yards when they stopped, waved and disappeared before my eyes.

The point in Brize Norton village where Chris Bromham saw the two children waiting to cross the road.

I am unable to offer any explanation for what happened that day, but I know there were two children, they did hold my hand and I watched as they walked away, then they just disappeared. Were they fulfilling a dream?, were they local?, and most disturbing of all, were they real or phantoms? These questions and many more went through my mind that day. Chris has since died, so we shall never be able to get a clearer view of his experiences that December day.

CHAPTER FIVE

SUPERNATURAL EVENTS IN:

CHARLBURY, FINSTOCK, LANGLEY, ASTHALL AND LEAFIELD

'The Broad Light Ghost'

The troop of horsemen, led by the Earl of Leicester, cantered up the beautiful avenue leading to the mansion at Cornbury Park. The Broad-Light, as this wide bordered, tree lined avenue was known, looked at its best in early spring, not the sort of place which you would associate with death and the haunting presence of a ghost.

However, the horsemen were brought to an abrupt halt when the figure of a woman appeared in the centre of the avenue, she appeared as if from nowhere, as the Earl drew closer, his face turned ashen white and shaking like a leaf he turned to his retainers and said in a shocked voice, "'Tis Amy". As it turned out, it was indeed Amy Robsart, or more correctly the ghost of Amy, wife of the Earl of Leicester, favourite of Queen Elizabeth the First. The manor built at what is now Cornbury Park was in the possession of the Earl, and he, along with the nobles of the day utilised the great house when hunting in Wychwood forest.

Leicester, a dashing young nobleman was a firm favourite of Elizabeth the First, it was even suspected that the Queen and the Earl were secret lovers and that the only obstacle to their joining in marriage was the Earl's wife Amy. Whatever the truth behind the rumours that circulated at the time, it was certainly true that Amy Robsart was an extremely unhappy woman having been almost totally neglected by her ambitious young husband.

Amy met her death under suspicious circumstances and it was widely rumoured that her husband was responsible for her untimely end, by throwing her down a flight of stairs at Cumnor Place. Whatever the circumstances surrounding Amy's death, her ghost has often appeared on the Broad-Light, but there is a pattern to the sightings and anyone unfortunate enough to see this unmistakable Elizabethan figure will, according to local folklore, be dead within ten days. The Earl of Leicester's retainer reported that immediately following her fatal fall, Amy's ghost had appeared before his master, the Earl, and informed him that, he would be joining her within ten days. Sure enough, nine days following the sighting, the Earl died from a mysterious and undiagnosed illness.

The story handed down through the ages is that Amy only appears to those in imminent danger and anyone spotting the Broad-Light Phantom will be dead within ten days. It should however be known that several people have reported sightings and lived to tell the tale. Could it be that Amy has mellowed with age, or perhaps she is now fully occupied, dealing with her errant husband.

The Phantom Coach from Charlbury

The phantom coach and four which runs from Charlbury, passing through Finstock and journeying on to goodness knows where, appears to follow a route more or less in line with the existing road, but at varying points on its journey the coach detours off this road to steer a course of its own. We do not know why this ghostly vehicle follows such a route, it appears most likely that the ancient road or staging posts once existed, at the points where the coach departs from the track of the current road.

The former owner of a riding school, just outside Charlbury, on the Charlbury, Finstock Road, reportedly witnessed the phantom coach wheeling past the entrance to his stables. This sighting was preceded by the distinctive sounds of horse and carriage, the entire spectacle remaining invisible with only the clatter of hooves and the rumbling of a carriage receding into the distance. Only after the sounds were heard was the coach sighted, disappearing round a bend in the road and hell bent for Finstock.

Another story from Charlbury tells of a number of Charlburians placing a barricade on the path taken by the phantom coach. Apparently the coach, or the sounds given off by the coach, stopped upon encountering the obstacles, whereupon it made the return journey to Charlbury only to start out again, once the barricade had been removed.

A rather chilling tale, and a most unusual one, because rarely has the coach been sighted, concerns a mother and her young son in an encounter on that part of the road just prior to reaching the bridge leading into Finstock.

It appeared that mother and son were returning home when they heard the sound of a coach and horses behind them, so they hastened to the side of the road but as nothing could be seen they crossed the bridge, when upon arriving at the other side, the boy startled his mother by saying, "That lady in the carriage wants me to go over to her". The boy's mother could see no sign of coach or horses, yet the unmistakable sound of hooves scraping and stamping on the ground was clearly heard. The boy seemed quite unconcerned at the turn events had taken and was quite ready to go and see what the lady wanted. His mother, by now quite terrified, grabbed his hand and made him stay exactly where he was. Suddenly the sound of coach and horses once more on the move could be clearly heard, the sound remained discernible for some time until it gradually faded into the distance.

The bridge on the road to Finstock where the phanom coach has been seen on numerous occasions.

Following this extraordinary encounter, the young boy was asked to describe what he had seen. "The lady was sitting in a green carriage, she wore a big hat with feathers in it, I could only see the top half of the lady and she was wearing a black jacket with a white blouse beneath. There were two men on the carriage, they were both dressed in brown with long boots, one had a whip and was sitting on the side fathest away from me, they both had hats on". The boy went on to tell how the lady had beckoned him over to the carriage and that she had been crying; he said she put both hands out to him and looked really angry when his mother wouldn't let him go.

THE FINSTOCK PHANTOMS

According to local folk lore, a huge creature, usually seen as a shadow, haunts Finstock. The monster has been observed by a number of people and apart from some minor detail all appear to have seen the same thing. The creature has been described as a cross between a broad shouldered, hairy neanderthal and a huge brown bear. At differing times the mystical beast has been seen shambling around back gardens in Finstock. This shadow phantom appears to be connected with ancient stone sculptures found in the area, fashioned into the shape of an animal unknown to nature. Unusual sightings of similar animals to this have been made in Ireland, Wales and Cornwall. Not surprisingly perhaps, similar ancient stone sculptures have also been found in these areas!

An early nineteenth century clergyman has often been seen on the road leading to the church, dressed in black and wearing the clergyman's garb of the period. This ancient vicar has been seen on several occasions slowly melting into a misty haze, as he walks unconcernedly through the gates and into hedgerows. Perhaps he is looking for the ghostly white stallion, which gallops freely along the main Finstock road, which apparition has been observed in 1996 and 1997, on both occasions, around the area of Hilltop Nurseries. The 1996 sighting was made as the horse seemingly left the entrance to the nurseries and galloped away up the hill, only to disappear half way up. The 1997 sighting was almost a reverse of the same event, the white horse appearing from nowhere near the bottom of the hill and again disappearing somewhere near the nursery entrance. Could this spectral white horse have escaped from a troop of horsemen seen galloping across fields close to

The road which now provides the entrance to Hill Top Nurseries. Site of encounters with the White Stallion.

Worsham, their white plumed broad brimmed hats and dashing appearance indicating mounted Cavaliers in pursuit of Cromwell's Roundheads ? Alternatively, the ghostly horse could be part of the phantom Charlbury to Finstock coach, although there have been no reports of loose horses being associated with this phenomenon.

THE LANGLEY TALES

Langley, which is not far from Leafield, is the site of what was once a hunting lodge, built by Prince John, and called Langley Palace, which acted as the temporary residence of visiting royalty on their hunting trips to Wychwood Forest. King Henry the Eighth, Mary Queen of Scots, and Queen Elizabeth the First, were just three of the many Kings and Queens who used the palace. Wychwood Forest was a favourite royal hunting ground for many years. A farm now stands on the site of Langley Palace.

A sad tale was recounted to me by Bette Hogben, a lady steeped in local fork-lore and now living at Church View in Witney. Bette tells of the time she and her family experienced a supernatural visitation from the past, when although she was only a young girl at the time, she remembers vividly every detail of that strange encounter and here is her story.

At the time of Bette's tale, the home in which she lived was situated in a row of cottages which belonged to the farm which stands on the site of Langley Palace, the cottage being approximately half a mile from the site. Bette's father and grandfather were uprooting a tree stump when they unearthed a large flat stone, beneath which was found an iron grid. Her father together with her grandfather and brother, managed to lift both the stone and the grid clear, which was quite a job as they were both very heavy objects. Having moved both pieces and a quantity of rubble, they then discovered an iron door. It took quite some time before they had cleared the area around the door sufficiently to allow it to open, then found crow-bars and levered it open, by which time it was too dark to carry out further investigations and there was an awful smell coming from a tunnel which the forcing open of the door had revealed. The family decided to wait until a more propitious time before investigating the secrets of their discovery, so the iron door was left open and the place remained unexplored for two to three days. Needless to say the young Bette could not contain her impatience and visited the site the very next day, when she observed that the door was black, studded and had what appeared to be two spy holes, positioned approximately three feet up from the bottom. The stench which had emanated from the tunnel had by now completely dispersed. Bette rushed off to inform her mother of what she had found, but all she was concerned about was that Bette stay well away from the site until her father had investigated the place further.

The evening following the discovery of the secret passage, Bette's mother was in the garden of their cottage hanging out the wash, when as she turned to make her way indoors she saw a hooded figure emerging from the underground passage. This figure walked unhurriedly toward her, moving slightly to the right as it came nearer. Bette explained that her mother, recounting the tale to her later, told her that the figure was that of a woman, wearing a long black hooded cloak with a thick green cord tied around her waist, drawing the cloak tightly about her body. The features were clearly visible and they were that of a middle aged woman, her eyes were clear blue and she had a wide mouth, aquiline nose, and strands of brown hair streaked with grey peeping from under her hood. The feature, however, which really struck Bette's mother was the unmistakable look of anguish and fear upon the lady's face. Bette's mother was to return again and again to that look, later explaining to Bette that she felt no fear for herself, just a terrible anxiety for the woman and a wave of hopelessness for her plight, whatever that was to be, or had been.

This spectral being appeared to three other members of the family, Bette's father, grandfather and Bette herself, when all with the exception of Bette, experienced the same feeling of despair. However the message passed to that small girl from the lady in the cloak was simple, "Put everything as it was and let me rest."

The family were in no doubt, following a meeting gathered round the kitchen table, that the iron door should be closed and sealed, the earth and rubble shovelled back into the hole, then the iron grid together with the flat stone placed in exactly the same spot from whence they had been removed. The family duly returned the site to its original condition and upon completion Bette's grandfather said a short prayer over the spot; the lady was never seen again.

Bette described to me the area where once she and her family lived, in the row of three cottages once owned by the farmer who rented them out. Bette is convinced that she could return to the spot and locate the hidden passage, meanwhile the current residents are unaware that they are literally walking over an ancient mystery each time they cross their lawn.

Another tale which many locals regard as a myth but which Bette insists is true, is the story of the burial party who lost a coffin containing a body, in Wychwood Forest. Bette's grandfather was a carter and it was he who was charged with the responsibility of carrying a young woman's body from Charlbury to Leafield for burial, it was mid winter and heavy snowfalls had occurred in the area. Snow was still falling when the burial party decided to carry on transporting the unfortunate woman's body to its final resting place, as the burial was planned to take place that day. Bette recalls how the people of Leafield and the surrounding villages were master poachers, indeed for some it was a way of life. Apparently the bearers of the coffin were travelling straight through the forest, it being the shortest route from Charlbury to Leafield, when they spotted a deer. Without a moment's hesitation the coffin was lowered to the ground and the whole group set off, through thick swirling snow, in pursuit of the deer. Bette recalls quite clearly listening to her grandfather describing the incident to the whole family the day after it happened. She recalls being told the hunting/burial party had returned to the place where they thought they had left the coffin but were unable to trace either hide or hair of it. The coffin had sunk into the drifting snow and fresh falls had completely obliterated all signs of it. Some four days were to elapse, following that fateful hunt, before the snow had thawed sufficiently for the coffin to be retrieved from its temporary resting place in Wychwood Forest.

The Foxy Lady of Leafield

When you consider that the majority of West Oxfordshire inns date back to the sixteenth, seventeenth and eighteenth centuries it is little wonder that these hostelries, some tucked away in villages and hamlets, have many a tale to tell, a haunting to experience and an atmosphere very specific to this corner of old England.

The inns have been used as staging posts for travellers, as meeting places and focal points of village life, strangers have passed through, some leaving a part of themselves others taking more than they left behind. All the comings and goings, politics and intrigues of generations have conspired to create an atmosphere unique in itself. One such place is 'The Fox' at Leafield, whose landlady and landlord, Anne and Shaun Doyle, have recognised the importance of retaining the three hundred years of atmosphere created by the personalities passing through The Fox, and they in turn have added their own blend of warmth and humour to this sixteenth century inn.

Open fires, 'space to breathe' between tables, lovely home cooked food and well kept beers all combine to create a welcoming atmosphere at this inn, which was once in the heart of Wychwood Forest.

There is a very special lady who resides at The Fox, dressed in a black cloak and sporting some very expensive riding boots this 'Foxy Lady' comes and goes as she pleases, sometimes seen as a shadow passing through the original wall adjacent to the old

The Fox at Leafield residence of The Foxy Lady, where her lover was murdered by her enraged husband.

fireplace, other times seen as a solid figure upstairs in the pub's living quarters, the 'Foxy Lady' wears a haughty expression as she glides through solid objects, on her way to who knows where, always in a hurry the apparition also leaves a faint hint of perfume in her wake.

It has been suggested that this is the spirit of a lady whose lover was killed about two hundred and fifty years ago. Apparently the lady's husband was aware that his wife had taken a lover and after spinning her a story that he would be gone for two days, he set a trap for them. 'The Fox', was the lovers' trysting place, so the husband sprung his trap and murdered his wife's lover in what is now the main bedroom of the inn where the wife later arrived, only to find her lover's lifeless body. She returned to her husband, but was unable to live with the knowledge that her husband had murdered the man she loved. The 'Foxy Lady' committed suicide in Wychwood Forest and her restless spirit sometimes returns to the old inn, vainly seeking her lost love.

A soft rustling sound and a rapid drop in temperature give warning of the impending arrival of the 'Foxy Lady'. This together with the faint waft of perfume as she passes by, are the signs which indicate her presence. One sighting of this glamorous phantom took place during lunch hour in the bar of 'The Fox'. At approximately twelve forty five, the landlord, Shaun, and two of his customers experienced a sudden chill in the air, which was unusual as both fires were burning cheerily. Then all three witnessed a shadow flow from the house side of the bar, through the counter, float over to the fire nearest the bar and disappear through the solid wall. The faint smell of lavender lingered in the bar for a few moments, then as the aroma dissipated the temperature returned to normal. Several other people in the bar at the same time failed to see the apparition. Shaun and Anne have no problem in living with the 'Foxy Lady, in fact apart from the sudden chills, there is an endearing quality about her presence which strikes a rapport in both mine hosts and those lucky enough to witness her 'passing through'.

Lucifer's Quest

According to local fork-lore, each and every seven years, the Devil rides out into the West Oxfordshire countryside, his quest being to acquire as many souls as possible to increase the population of Hades. The Devil's favourite hunting ground appears to be in and around Wychwood Forest, or those places cloaked by this once

A beautiful shot of Wychwood on a bright summer day. The wood does not always appear this welcoming.

A highly evocative picture of Wychwood in winter. A stark contrast to the summer scene, and much less welcoming.

great, dark dense and secret forest. For the benefit of those now living within the old area occupied by the forest and who may not be aquainted with the Satanic sorties, a description of Lucifer and his demonic coach follows. Needless to say however, if you see either or both, it may well already be too late !

The coach is a black closed four wheeler, highly polished and drawn by two chestnut horses, on either door there is a red crest and the spokes of the wheels are blood red. Two coachmen sit high up on the front of the vehicle, each dressed in full length black coats, with white stockings, very shiny brown riding boots and black tricorn hats. They are both immaculately turned out and the pair are described as being strikingly handsome, with dark saturnine features.

Sometimes Lucifer can be seen seated inside the coach, while on other occasions, red tasselled curtains conceal the occupant from human gaze. Lucifer himself has been described as a truly imposing figure, being over six feet in height, slim of build, darkly handsome and with a wide and demonic smile.

How many souls he has bought over the centuries can only be a matter of conjecture; however as he has been visiting this particular region on a regular basis for over three hundred years, he must find it profitable to continue his forays into the Cotswold countryside.

There is a much believed tale in the Wychwood area, of a bold gypsy who raced the Devil through Wychwood. The starting point was in Finstock and the finishing point a tree sacred to the 'Green Man', ancient spirit of the forest, which was situated in the centre of Wychwood. The bargain twixt the Devil and the gypsy was that, should the gypsy win he would receive a solid gold bowl, should the Devil win he would take and keep the soul of the gypsy. The story tells how the Devil became trapped, some say in a bog, others that it was in quicksand, from which the gypsy rescued him and as a result, won the golden bowl and at the same time, extracted a promise from the Devil, never to pester the gypsy race again. Legend has it that the Devil, however diabolical he may be, always keeps his word.

Lucifer scours the world in his quest for more souls to join his legion of damned souls and in the areas around Wychwood, he seems to have been particularly successful in Finstock, Charlbury, Chipping Norton, Old Minster, Shipton, Ascot, Shilton, Leafield and many of the other villages and hamlets which once nestled in and around the forest.

CHAPTER SIX

SUPERNATURAL EVENTS IN:

BURFORD

Can there be a more delightful place than Burford, 'the town on a hill'? Beautifully positioned as the 'Gateway to The Cotswolds', it represents all that is precious to the people of West Oxfordshire. Bordered by the Windrush, that ancient river which flows into Old Father Thames, and with the two thousand year old Wychwood Forest, on its doorstep, Burford is a veritable gem in the crown that is England.

The lovely church of St John the Baptist, full of 'nooks and crannies', with its tower clock still driven by weights and where the visitor can see tombs, memorials, a font carrying the name of levellers who were taken from the church, which acted as a temporary prison during the Cromwellian period, and shot. There are ancient tombstones, telling of surgeons' wives, barbers, gentry, knights and commoners now long dead, and before you leave the church, linger awhile to look at the tomb of Sir Lawrence and Lady Tanfield, study their effigies lying atop their tomb and try to relate their appearance to this strange tale of Burford.

The Windrush, The Bottle, The Cloud and Lady Tanfield

Sir Lawrence and Lady Tanfield, both of whom are lying beneath that elegant tomb in the church of St John the Baptist, were, during their lifetime in Burford, the two most loathed people ever to walk the streets of that Cotswold town, she in particular is remembered as being the 'epitome of evil'. Whole families were evicted without a second thought if it suited the evil pair's purpose, tenants were constantly threatened and floggings were frequently inflicted upon servants and tenants for the most trivial offences. Even relatives were exploited, hence they never stayed long within that corrupt household. There were suspicious circumstances surrounding the death of Sir Lawrence. Lady Tanfield herself conducted everything

The tomb of Sir Lawrence and Lady Tanfield, inside St John the Baptists Church, Burford. In life they were both loathed and detested by the people of Burford. Courtesy of St. John The Baptist Church.

to do with his death and subsequent burial, in great haste. Among other things, no doctor was summoned to minister to Sir Lawrence, who had died quite suddenly and unexpectedly. Eventually Lady Tanfield followed her husband and went the way of all mortals, or so the good people of Burford believed at the time of her death. However they were not to be left in peace, for the ghosts of their oppressors returned following Lady Tanfield's burial, to continue their reign of fear among the good folk of the town.

The Tanfields were aware of the mistrust and hatred the townsfolk of Burford had for them, for they unhesitatingly exploited everyone they came in contact with. There was talk of witchcraft and sorcery surrounding the couple, the thin, malevolent, pinched face of Lady Tanfield together with her predictions of the terrible fate awaiting the locals upon her death, did little to dispel the townsfolk's fears and tended to confirm the witchcraft rumours. One of Lady Tanfield's stated aims was to decimate the entire population of Burford, her remark that she "Would like to grind the people of Burford to powder beneath the wheels of my chariot", began to take on a sinister meaning, when a fiery chariot was seen flying over the town with the hated lady Tanfield at the reins.

Sometimes she was accompanied by Sir Lawrence, but more often than not the infernal vehicle was occupied by the malevolent Lady Tanfield alone. The chariot began making more and more appearances, accompanying the frightful pair and often acting as though it had a mind of its own, also a small dark cloud would sometimes be seen with them, it was said that should this cloud

A carved skeleton which lies beneath the Tanfield Tomb in St John The Baptist's Church, Burford.

envelop you, your mind would be 'sucked out' and you would be rendered insane. I have been told by a recent ex-member of the Burford Boy Scout group, that this 'dark cloud' was a frequent subject of conversation both at the old scout hut and also around their camp fires; it was even in recent times a subject taken quite seriously among the boys.

The frequency of sightings reached an all time high in the late seventeen hundreds and it was during this period that the clergy finally decided to take action to rid the town of this spectral nuisance. A number of them, the figure varies between four and seven, met with 'bell, book and candle', intent upon the imprisonment of 'The malevolence that was lady Tanfield'. A 'blessed bottle', was used in which to trap the demon spirit and having accomplished this the 'blessed bottle' was corked, sealed and hurled from the bridge into the river Windrush, where it landed and became lodged under the third arch. Local folklore has it that should there be a drought and the Windrush under the bridge run dry, then Lady Tanfield will resume her low flying raids over the rooftops of Burford. There have been occasions when the locals have prevented that particular arch under the bridge from drying out by adding bucketsful of water to the spot where the 'blessed bottle' is said to have become lodged.

Not Any Old Tom, Dick or Harry

The Dunstan boys, Tom, Dick and Harry hailed from Fulbrook, over the Burford bridge where turning right will bring you to Fulbrook. The Dunstan's were a much respected family in the neighbourhood and it is not known why the three sons turned to a life of crime. Perhaps it was the temptation of easy pickings and a veritable labyrinth of bolt-holes in and around Wychwood Forest, which made highway robbery appear an easier way of life than farming. The three men started a crime wave which had repercussions as far away as London. Set a thief to catch a thief, the old saying goes and that is what the authorities eventually did. Four well known foot-pads being hired, to track down and bring to justice the Dunstan brothers. The four ex-criminals took lodgings in Burford and proceeded to set about laying traps for Tom, Dick and Harry. However the Dunstan's planned each robbery down to the finest detail and their knowledge of the locality was such, that it was said they knew every nook and cranny of Wychwood Forest and not even a pack of hounds could find them once they had 'gone to earth' there.

One old story much repeated, has the Dunstans shoeing their horses back to front in order to confuse their would-be trackers, and whatever they did they were certainly very successful in evading capture, until one night around seventeen sixty. The three men, following an unsuccessful attempt to rob the stage-coach, made a dash for one of their bolt holes, in this instance Langley Hall. However they had been working with a gang of cut-throats from Woodstock and one of the members of this gang had informed on them to the authorities. Details of how, when and where the robbery was to take place plus information as to where the gang would make for to divide the loot, was passed to the authorities who secretly placed their men both in Langley Hall and near the route of the intended robbery. The Dunstans detected the ambush, aborted the robbery and raced hell for leather to what they thought was a safe haven, unfortunately for them a second ambush at the Hall was sprung and in the ensuing melee Dick had his arm severed. Reports said that his brothers had cut off Dick's arm when he was trapped in the door leading into Langley Hall, but this is to be doubted. Whatever happened that night the three brothers made good their escape but poor Dick was never seen again; some say he died of his wounds and was secretly buried in Wychwood forest by his brothers. We shall never know the truth of the tale from any man or woman, and the forest will not readily give up its secrets. Tom and Harry carried on their life of crime until one fateful February night in seventeen sixty seven, the pair were apprehended over what started out as a trivial matter but which ended up seeing them both hanged.

A hostelry known as Capps Lodge, not far from Burford, was a notorious meeting place for highwaymen and the seamier inhabitants of the local parishes. It appears that on the fateful February night in seventeen sixty seven, a fight broke out at the inn between the brothers and one William Harding, who was employed as a serving man and who was hit by one of the brothers for listening in to their conversation. The owner of the inn joined in the fisticuffs and a general melee ensued, ending up outside the hostelry where Harding was shot and fatally wounded. The brothers Dunstan were promptly apprehended, swiftly tried, found guilty of murder and sentenced to be hanged.

The brothers were duly hanged on what was known as 'Hangman's Tree'. This was an ancient oak on the edge of Wychwood Forest, which alas is no longer there, but not so long ago you could visit the tree whereon the initials "TD and HD 1767" had been carved. Apparently the Dunstans were exhibited in a gibbet on the old oak until predators had picked their bones clean, and people from miles around journeyed to see the gruesome sight.

If you are travelling in the Swinbrook, Fordwells, Asthall areas you may catch a glimpse of the two one time notorious highwaymen, as they sit beneath what was their final earthly resting place, an old oak tree which has since been felled, but which once stood in stark loneliness in the middle of a field between Fordwells and Swinbrook.

The Haunted Priory Burford

There is a diminutive figure which can occasionally be seen ringing a non existent bell at 2.00am in the grounds of what used to be Burford priory.

This little man with the nut brown complexion is a monk, garbed in a garment but a few shades darker than his face. 'The Little Monk', is seen on a regular basis and on each occasion, at or about two o clock in the morning, he solemnly tolls the priory bell. There is a look upon his face and an aura of deep sadness surrounding this apparition, as he walks around what was the grounds and what has become the ruins of the ancient priory. Several local people have witnessed his passing through the walls of more recent structures, to the accompaniment of the sound of dolorous chanting. All the witnesses attest to an overwhelming sensation of grief and sadness while witnessing the sad passage of 'The Little Monk'. The tolling of the bell at two in the morning indicates that an event of great import had taken place within the Priory. An event such as the death of a particularly beloved Prior would cause the bell to be tolled at such an hour, immediately following his death and the sad loss of such a saintly leader must have deeply affected all within the priory. It is quite possible that the spirit of 'The Little Monk', overburdened with grief, cannot bring himself to leave and is doomed forever to signal his distress by tolling the bell at the hour of the beloved Prior's death.

The area both within and around the Priory also appears to be well endowed with transitory and non monastic phantoms. One of the more persistent being the figure of an elderly gentleman dressed in 'old fashioned', clothes and carrying a flintlock musket can be seen in various parts of the Priory. The passing of this ghost, seemingly on sentry duty, has been witnessed at various times, but the majority of sightings have occurred during the late evening in the month of October. I have been unable to discover much more about this military phantom, apart from the fact that on one occasion, an American couple saw him so clearly that they were moved to speak to him, whereupon he promptly disappeared, probably frightened off by the strangeness of their accents.

Upton's Battle

Just outside Burford a pitched battle between the tribes of the two kingdoms of Wessex and Mercia took place during the turbulent times following the departure of Roman rule from these islands. As was always the case in those ancient times, the fighting was both fierce and predominantly hand to hand. This combat between the men of Wessex and Mercia resulted in particularly heavy loss of life on both sides. These losses occurred both during the battle, and in a great many cases, immediately after, when the wounds inflicted by dirty weapons or through filthy clothing, set infections raging unchecked through the bodies of the wounded, leaving only the slenderest chance of recovery and most often bringing about agonising and lingering deaths for a great many of the wounded. The site where this particular contest took place has ever since been known as 'Battle Edge', which is situated near Upton.

Several reports from witnesses record apparent re-enactments of the struggle, taking place upon 'Battle Edge'. Subsequent research has established that no Local or National re-enactment society has been involved in such an event on this site. Similarly, permission has not been sought or granted to stage such a large re-enactment. There is no doubt that the battle was considered at the time and right down to the present day, to be of great significance to the people of Burford, who celebrate the event every summer, when during the annual festive parade, a golden dragon which is emblematic of the battle is paraded through the streets.

The phantoms fighting on the banks of the Windrush, bear a remarkable resemblance to the frequent sightings at Edge Hill, where Roundheads and Cavaliers, long since dead of their wounds, from which they will have suffered and died in a similarly agonising manner to their ancient forebears, return from the grave to re-enact their last hours of full and active life before being cut down in their last battle.

CHAPTER SEVEN

SUPERNATURAL EVENTS IN:

SHIPTON UNDER WYCHWOOD

Sebastian at the Shaven Crown

A fourteenth century inn, unique in the fact that it is one of the ten oldest Inns in England, with the added distinction of never having closed, stands proudly in the village of Shipton under Wychwood. 'The Shaven Crown' has a further unique feature, brother Sebastian the ghost of a long dead monk. I visited the bedroom where Sebastian resides and I can understand why the old monk appears to be happy with his lot. Room eleven is a large airy comfortable room containing a huge four poster bed, windows giving splendid views across to the church, ancient oak furniture and the most unusual chandelier I have ever seen, all of which combine to make an irresistible combination. Like Sebastian, I would cheerfully stay there for a few hundred years!

The first intimation that the new owners, Robert and Jane Burpitt, had of Sebastian's presence, was when Robert attended to the locking of the large gates at the rear of the hotel. On walking back through the courtyard he was astonished to hear what appeared to be the chanting of monks, which he put down to his own over active imagination, until a light illuminated the courtyard, revealing what appeared to be the outline or figure of a monk, fully robed and cowled.

Robert is a cynic when it comes to things supernatural and he readily and happily explains this when discussing such matters, but as he gets into the subject you realise that there is no doubt in his mind that he experienced something almost spiritual and definitely other worldly that night. Jessie Rainbow, who had been employed at the inn for some forty years, has no doubt at all as to the presence of Sebastian; Jessie will not remain in room eleven unless the door stays wide open whilst she is in there.

Other remarkable occurrences have taken place, Jessie has been summoned by name, quite sharply, when she has been late for

The Shaven Crown 'Sebastian's Room' is within the circle. Photograph by kind permission of Robert and Jane Burpitt.

The interior of Sebastian's room.

lunch, the problem is that the voice is disembodied. An invisible dog has been heard growling in the inn and many guests down through the years have commented on the old monk seen ascending the stairs or walking the corridors.

One thing is certain a visit to this delightful inn is a must, painstakingly restored by the present owners Robert and Jane, an irresistible combination of delicious food, fine wines, a good selection of beers and a charming ghost, all combine to ensure that even the most discerning guest enjoys a delightful stay at the 'Shaven Crown'.

The fact that bedroom number eleven was once a chapel which was utilised by the monks of nearby Bruern Abbey, reinforces the theory that it is a monk who has been seen and not a cloaked lady as some guests have claimed. More recent history has seen the 'Shaven Crown' used as a clandestine meeting place by Oswald Mosley, leader of the British pro-Nazi 'Black Shirts', and one of the Mitford girls who lived nearby. Similarly, village folk lore insists that Adolf Hitler also used the inn as a trysting place with the Mitford girls.

Inside The Shaven Crown. Sebastian's staircase, a black dog sometimes also appears here.

Whatever has taken place in the far or near past there will always be a warm and hospitable welcome at this ancient inn. Incidentally opposite the 'Shaven Crown' stands a monument to the seventeen people of Shipton under Wychwood who sadly perished whilst seeking a better life in New Zealand. The ship carrying the immigrants was *The Cospatrick*, which sank with all hands in 1874. The stone fountain which stands on the Green at Shipton, was erected to their memory and in 1974 a beech tree, still standing, was planted to commemorate the one hundredth anniversary of the sinking of *The Cospatrick*.

CHAPTER EIGHT

SUPERNATURAL EVENTS IN:

FARINGDON

The Phantom Lady Rides Out

A young lady once living at Field Assarts, and now residing at Lidstone, witnessed an extraordinary happening as she was returning to her home at Field Assarts. It was a late October evening in nineteen ninety six when the incident occurred. Tracy had just left Faringdon by car and had travelled about a mile, it was a fine evening and just turning dark when she was heading towards Clanfield and she spotted a single flickering light coming towards her on her side of the road. It was obvious to Tracy that the light was not emanating from any motor vehicle but it was nevertheless extremely disconcerting to have, whatever it was, coming directly towards her on the wrong side of the road. I shall let Tracy take up the story in her own words.

'I thought to myself, what the hell is this idiot playing at, if he doesn't stop soon he'll be right into me, I decided that discretion was the better part of valour and I pulled right into the left side of the road, as far as I could without going into the ditch. It had been raining earlier and I wasn't too happy about getting stuck in the mud. I was undecided as to whether or not I should put my car's headlights onto high beam, if I left them on high I might blind whoever it was, so I gave a quick flick onto high beam then immediately back onto dipped, I felt that should be sufficient warning to the idiot to get back onto his half of the road. As the light approached it appeared to be surrounded by a black mass, there was no discernible shape to the mass until it got to about fifty yards in front of me, then I could see that it was a carriage pulled by a single horse and with a woman driver, the light I could now see quite clearly was a lantern in which a flickering candle burned.

The woman driver could be clearly seen as the carriage was an open vehicle, she looked neither to the left nor right, the only movement was when she gave the horse a light flick with a whip which she appeared to take from the side of the carriage. I knew instantly that I was witnessing something supernatural, neither the horse nor carriage made any sound and the entire right hand side of the vehicle passed clean through my car from front to back. I allowed the rig to carry on for about twenty to thirty yards and then I got out of my car and watched as horse, carriage and driver vanished up the road to goodness knows where.'

ACKNOWLEDGEMENTS

Acknowledgements and thanks to the following for allowing me into their homes, their business premises and for sharing their experiences with me.

David Parsons, Unwins, High Street, Witney
Len and Arthur Tooley of Witney
Ken Cook of Witney
Janet and Gerald Webb, Long Hanborough
Bette Hogben of Witney
Steve Thompson and Diana Rose, 'The Angel', Witney
Shaun and Anne Doyle, 'The Fox', Leafield
Robert and Jane Burpitt, 'The Shaven Crown', Shipton under Wychwood
J.P.H. Lord of Long Hanborough
Alan Bennett of Headington, Oxford

Acknowledgements to J.A. Giles *History of Witney*.

Acknowledgements to West Oxon Tourist Board and their Visitor Information Centres for their friendly advice, help and the district map.

Acknowledgements and thanks to Witney and District Historical Society. The Society's *A Walk Round Witney* is essential reading for both locals and tourists.

Acknowledgements and thanks to Barrie Rogers for his map. The booklet *Minster Lovell, An Historical Guide* is an absolute gem.

Photography by Terry Mead and Tiff Martin.

Dear Reader,

Now that you have read this book, you may feel moved to think that you would like to write, or perhaps you have already written, a Local History book yourself.

If this is the case, why not write to us requesting further information on the presentation of Local History material, for possible publication.

We can supply you with introductory information on the most likely subjects to be published and the most effective manner in which to present your material, in order to achieve the best possible chance for your work to be considered by the editor.

Our information also includes guidance on the selection and handling of photographs and other illustrative material, including the crucial matter of choosing the most appropriate and eye catching cover illustration.

Finally I think it important to advise you that by far the majority of authors whose work we publish, have never been previously published!

For further information regarding writing Local History publications, please write to me at the address shown below.
I look forward to hearing from you.

Yours sincerely,

Mike Parsons

Mike Parsons.
Imprint Manager.
Wharncliffe Books.

Mike Parsons, Wharncliffe Books, 47 Church Street, Barnsley, South Yorkshire, S70 2AS.